HINDUISM

Frequently Asked Questions

RELATED TITLES PUBLISHED

BY CHINMAYA MISSION®

Hindu Culture: An Introduction

The Holy Geeta

In Indian Culture, Why Do We . . .

Meditation & Life

Self-Unfoldment

Tattva Bodha

THE HINDU CULTURE SERIES

HINDUISM

Frequently Asked Questions

CENTRAL CHINMAYA MISSION TRUST

Publishers

Central Chinmaya Mission Trust

Saki Vihar Road, Powai, Mumbai 400 072, India

(91-22) 2857-2367; www.chinmayamission.com; ccmt@vsnl.com

Chinmaya Mission West

P.O. Box 129, Piercy, CA 95587, USA

(1-707) 247-3488; www.chinmayamission.org; secretary@chinmayamission.org

Chinmaya Publications

560 Bridgetown Pike, Langhorne, PA 19053, USA

(1-215) 396-0390; www.chinmayamission.org; publications@chinmayamission.org

Credits

Cover Image of Mother Durga: Courtesy of Truth Consciousness

www.truthconsciousness.org, © 1990 Truth Consciousness

Cover Design: Bhaskar Raman, Odalis Valdivieso

Printed by Jak Printers Pvt Ltd; jakprint@vsnl.com

Jak Compound, Dadaji Kondeo Cross Lane, Byculla (East), Mumbai 400 027, India

Library of Congress Control Number: 2005909291

ISBN 1-880687-38-0

First Edition : August 2006 - 2000 copies

Reprint : January 2007 - 3000 copies

Reprint : May 2008 - 3000 copies

Reprint : July 2008 - 5000 copies

Price : Rs. 90.00

The Chinmaya Mission

The Chinmaya Mission, founded by His Holiness Swami Chinmayananda, is a global charitable organisation, dedicated to sharing the wisdom of Vedanta, the philosophical core of Hinduism, to all who seek it.

Vedanta addresses fundamental questions on the nature of happiness and the purpose of life. As such, it is a universal science, relevant to all people regardless of faith. Through the activities of the Chinmaya Mission, one can incorporate the knowledge of the Bhagavad Geeta and Upanishads into daily life, furthering one's own spiritual growth through service to society.

In the UK, the Chinmaya Mission is based in Hendon, London but conducts a diverse range of activities across the UK including :

- Lecture series on Vedanta
- Interactive discussion groups and classes
- Seminars and retreats
- Social projects
- Children's classes and GCSE's in Hinduism
- Classes for young people
- Meditation and yoga
- Devotional and cultural activities and celebrations
- Books, publications, CDs and DVDs

Further information can be found at www.chinmayauk.org and hundreds of books and educational materials on Vedanta can be purchased on-line at www.chinmayabooks.com

Chinmaya Mission UK
Chinmaya Kirti,
2 Egerton Gardens,
Hendon, London
NW4 4BA
Tel.: 020 8203 6288
E-mail: *info@chinmayauk.org*

CONTENTS

7. What are the two doctrines of karma and reincarnation, and why do Hindus believe in them?

8. What determines whether an act is a merit (*puṇya*) or a sin (*pāpa*)?

9. What is the Hindu concept of heaven and hell?

10. What are the goals of human life according to Hindu ethics?

11. What are the four *āshramas*, or stages, of an individual's life?

12. What is meant by "caste" in Hinduism?

13. What is the spiritual significance of joining one's palms in *namaskāra* or *namaste*?

14. What is the spiritual significance of the marks on the forehead of *bindi*, *tilak*, and *tripuṇḍra*?

15. Describe the two main categories of Hindu scriptures: *shruti* and *smriti*.

16. What does *veda* mean?

17. How many Vedas are there, what do they deal with, and what sections do they consist of?

18. What are the *Upa-vedas*, how many are there, and what do they deal with?

19. What are the *Vedāṅgas*?

20. What are the schools of Hindu philosophy?

21. What does *Vedānta* mean?

22. Does Vedantic philosophy include different schools of thought? If so, what are they?

23. How do we reconcile the different schools of philosophy and different approaches to the Truth?

24. What are the three main scriptural sources for a Vedantin?

25. What are the Upanishads?

26. How many Upanishads are there?

27. What are the great declarations, or *mahāvākya*s, and where are they found in the Vedas?

28. What are *sūtra*s?

29. What are the *Brahma Sūtra*s?

30. What is *Shrīmad Bhagavad Gītā*?

31. What are the *Purāṇa*s and how many are there?

32. What are the two major historical epics in Hinduism?

33. What is *Shrīmad Bhāgavatam*?

34. What is *Yoga Vāsishṭha*?

35. What are the *Dharma Shāstra*s, how many are there, and who wrote them?

36. Who is Manu and what is a *manvantara*, or the Hindu calculation of time?

51. What is a human being's external and internal composition?

52. Describe in detail the three bodies that make up a human being.

53. What is the *antaḥ-karaṇa*, or inner equipment?

54. What is the mind and what are its different aspects?

55. What are the waking, dream, and deep sleep states, and what is the state beyond time and space?

56. What is the BMI Chart?

57. Who is the *jīva*, who is *Īshvara*, and what is the relationship between the two?

58. What is *māyā*?

59. If the *jīva* is bound by *māyā*, yet is responsible for the choices that determine his destiny, how much of his life is fate and how much of it is free will?

60. If the *jīva* is the maker of his own destiny, is there any value in praying to *Īshvara*?

61. What is *Brahman*?

62. What additional terms, other than *Ātman* and *Brahman*, are used to indicate a human being's true nature?

63. What is spiritual liberation?

64. What causes an individual to consider himself bound?

65. How can the knowledge of the Self be imparted if the Self is not an object?

66. What is the difference between self-hypnotism and Self-realization?

67. What are three direct means of knowledge for Self-realization?

68. What is meditation?

69. How many kinds of votaries are there among those who seek God?

70. Who is a *yogī*?

71. What are the prescribed paths to reach the stage of a *yogī*?

72. Who is a guru?

73. Who is a disciple?

74. What are the qualifications of a spiritual seeker?

PART FIVE: WHY RELIGION? 79

75. Why does religion seem to appeal only to the minority?

76. What is meant by the statement "Hinduism is tolerant"?

77. What is the relationship between science and religion?

78. How do we discover why God created this world?

79. How does Vedanta help a person achieve happiness?

80. Is the influence of religion on the masses declining? If not, how can we account for corruption and other such pointers to widespread deterioration in ethical and moral values?

81. The traditional charge against Hinduism is that it is fatalistic and that it inhibits progress by making people slaves to the belief in the inevitability of whatever is to happen. How far is this true? What is the basis of such an accusation, which is being advanced even today by well-meaning and highly educated people?

82. It is said that the greatest strength of Hinduism is its breadth of outlook and that this is also its greatest weakness, in that there are very few common prescribed religious observances obligatory for all, as in other religions. Is it necessary and possible to outline certain basic, minimum observances for all Hindus?

83. Will the fundamental values of Hinduism be in any way affected by the eradication of casteism, toward which a concerted effort is being made now, on all levels? If Harijans, who constitute a sizable population among Hindus, are made to feel that their religion exposes them to ridicule, how are they to love that religion? In other words, how can all sections of Hindus be made to take equal interest in, and have the same sense of belonging to, their religion?

84. Hinduism has always renewed or revitalized itself according to the needs of the times. In today's context, are any corrective measures called for? If so, who will bring them about, and how can they be brought about and made acceptable to the masses?

85. Are fasting and such other dietary regulations necessary for leading a spiritual life? Is a guru essential for one to enter the spiritual path and attain the goal?

86. Will mantras lose their sanctity if they are not in Sanskrit? There are various *saṁskāra*s prescribed in Hinduism from birth to death. Many of these *saṁskāra*s are not being observed today. Should they not be revived?

87. What is the role of rituals in religion? Are they to be discouraged?

88. What is your view regarding proselytization? If you were convinced that Hinduism has a great role to play in the world, would you consider adopting proselytization?

89. Are changes visible in Hinduism's doctrines and in the modes of individual and collective worship as a result of contact with the West?

APPENDIX 95

Vedas

*Upa-Veda*s

*Darshana*s: Schools of Philosophy

*Shabda Shāstra*s

Arts and Sciences

*Pramāṇa*s: Means of Knowledge

108 Principal Upanishads

Sanskrit Pronunciation Guide

PREFACE

Chinmaya Mission® is pleased to release *Hinduism: Frequently Asked Questions* as a part of *The Hindu Culture Series*. This book is based on Chinmaya Mission's earlier publication, *Our Heritage* by R. S. Nathan (Swami Nityananda).

To help young students of Indian culture gain a better understanding of the glory of *Sanātana Dharma*, more commonly referred to today as Hinduism, in July 1967, Chinmaya Mission published a tri-monthly series of booklets entitled *Our Heritage*. Eventually, select topics and ten booklets, with most of the questions and answers authored by R. S. Nathan and a few compiled from various sources, were published as one volume.

His Holiness Swami Chinmayananda, the founder and head of Chinmaya Mission, impressed with the acclaimed publication, sent out 500 copies to Mission workers, devotees, and patrons in India and abroad. Though the series was mainly intended for Chinmaya Bala Vihar and Chinmaya Yuva Kendra (Chinmaya Mission's children's and youth wings, respectively), adults also found the information useful.

The information in this new reference text is vast, but by no means comprehensive. Suggested reading for further study has been included in some instances. Complementary works from Chinmaya Publications include *Hindu Culture: An Introduction*, *The Holy Geeta*, *Meditation & Life*, *Self-Unfoldment*, *Tattva Bodha* and *In Indian Culture Why Do We.*

We thank Rupali Gupta, Rudite Emir, Swami Advayananda, and the Chinmaya International Foundation for their time and effort in bringing out this new publication.

Chinmaya Mission West

Central Chinmaya Mission Trust

August 2006

CHINMAYA MISSION

Chinmaya Mission® was established in India in 1953 by devotees of Swami Chinmayananda. They formed the nucleus of a spiritual renaissance movement that now encompasses a wide range of spiritual, educational, and charitable activities, ennobling the lives of thousands in India and outside its borders. Administered by Central Chinmaya Mission Trust in Mumbai, India, the Mission is now headed by His Holiness Swami Tejomayananda.

Following the Vedic teacher-taught tradition (*guru-shishya paramparā*), Chinmaya Mission makes available the ageless wisdom of Vedanta, the knowledge of the one Reality, and provides the tools to realize that wisdom in one's life. "To give maximum happiness to the maximum number for the maximum time" is the tenet that drives Mission workers to uplift humanity beyond selfish and sectarian attitudes and activities. Each person's gain is manifold: personal growth, heightened efficiency, contentment, and the ability to live with others in peace and harmony.

For more information, see *Chinmaya Mission: Transforming Lives*, or visit www.chinmayamission.com

His Holiness Swami Chinmayananda, founder of Chinmaya Mission, taught spirituality as the art of living. Through *jñāna yoga* (the path of knowledge), he emphasized the balance of head and heart, pointing out selfless work, study, and meditation as the cornerstones of spiritual practice.

Not satisfied by worldly aspirations or his degrees in literature and law, Balakrishna Menon pursued spiritual studies for nine years in the Himalayas, under the guidance of Swami Sivananda and the tutelage of Swami Tapovanam. He eventually came to share this Vedantic knowledge with the masses, in the form of the dynamic teacher known as Swami Chinmayananda.

Swamiji is renowned worldwide as a spiritual master and one of the foremost teachers of *Shrīmad Bhagavad Gītā*. He is credited with the renaissance of spirituality and cultural values in India, and with the spreading of the ageless wisdom of *Advaita Vedānta*, as expounded by Ādi Shaṅkarāchārya, throughout the world.

Swami Chinmayananda attained *mahāsamādhi* in August 1993. His legacy remains in the form of written, audio, and video publications; social service projects; Vedanta teachers whom he taught and inspired; and Chinmaya Mission centers worldwide, serving the spiritual and cultural needs of local communities.

Additional biographical information can be found in *Journey of a Master*, *Ageless Guru*, *Swami Chinmayananda: A Life of Inspiration and Service*, and *At Every Breath, A Teaching*.

His Holiness Swami Tejomayananda, the present spiritual head of Chinmaya Mission worldwide, is fulfilling the vision that Swami Chinmayananda charted. As he puts it, "I am not in Swamiji's shoes; I am at His feet."

Swami Tejomayananda has served as *āchārya* (dean) of the *Sandeepany* institutes of Vedanta (*gurukula*s of Chinmaya Mission) in India, and as *āchārya* in Mission centers in India and the US. He has written commentaries on scriptural texts, translated Swami Chinmayananda's commentaries into Hindi, and authored a number of books. A key contribution is *Hindu Culture*: *An Introduction*, which has been acclaimed for its clear description of the basics of Hinduism and adopted as a reference text in some American high schools.

Swamiji excels in expounding upon a wide spectrum of Hindu scriptures, from *Rāmāyaṇa*, to *Shrīmad Bhagavad Gītā*, to the Upanishads. His easy manner, combined with his in-depth analyses and devotional renderings of Vedantic texts, have drawn many newcomers into the spiritual fold.

PART ONE

FUNDAMENTAL CONCEPTS

PART ONE: FUNDAMENTAL CONCEPTS

1. What is the aim of the Hindu religion?

The aim of the Hindu religion is Self-realization (*Ātma-jñāna*), or God-realization (*Brahma-jñāna*), the knowledge of Oneness. Various terms, all leading to the same goal of Oneness, can be used to state this aim:

- Intuition of the Reality: *Brahma-anubhava*
- Insight into the Truth: *Brahma-darshana*
- Contact with the Supreme: *Brahma-saṁsparsha*
- Direct apprehension of the Reality: *Brahma-sākshātkāra*

2. What is the Hindu concept of God?

God is *Brahman*, the One, the changeless Truth or Reality. As *Brahman* cannot be conceived by the intellect, it cannot be defined; it can only be indicated (see Question 61).

With respect to creation, God is the changeless Substratum supporting the changing universe. Example: The god of waves is the ocean; the god of ornaments is gold; the god of pots is mud; the god of shirts is cotton. God is thus the cause and the effect. The effect is nothing but the cause in another form. And if the cause is removed, the effect ceases to exist.

Hinduism also refers to God as the Trinity of Brahmā (the creator), Vishṇu (the sustainer), and Shiva (the destroyer). God is the supremely intelligent, ultimate Cause from which the entire universe has emerged, in which the universe exists, and into which it eventually dissolves.

It is important to note that Hinduism is not polytheistic (belief in many gods, each a separate entity). Based on varying schools of Hindu philosophy, Hinduism can be called as monotheistic (belief in one God, manifesting different powers in different forms, where there is a dualistic relationship between God and the individual) or monist (belief in one God expressing as all forms, where God alone is or Oneness alone is, and all of creation is but a manifestation of the one Reality).

3. Why is the Hindu religion called *Sanātana Dharma* and who founded it?

Sanātana means "eternal." *Dharma* is a word that defies exact translation in English or any other language, but can be said to mean "the values of life that sustain us." Therefore, *Sanātana Dharma* is that religion which is based on life's eternal (universal) values.

By its literal meaning alone, it is clear that *Sanātana Dharma* is not a religion founded by any historical figure. It is based on eternal truths—principles and values of life—that hold true for all people, in all places, at all times—past, present, and future.

4. Explain in detail the meaning of the word *dharma*.

In the progress of Indian philosophical thought, the word *dharma* has acquired such a comprehensive and complex significance that it is almost impossible to define or articulate it in any other language. One description of dharma is "the law of being." The essential characteristic of a thing, without which it cannot remain as that thing, is its dharma.

Example: The sweetness of sugar, the luminosity of the sun, the heat of fire, the coolness of water, and the divine spark of Existence in the human being.

Dharma can viewed on two levels—cosmic and individual. On the cosmic level, the dharma of totality is called *sanātana dharma*, which is eternal and common to all individuals, at all times. On the societal level, *sanātana dharma* translates into a code of fundamental values that govern our daily lives (see Question 35). On the individual level, a person's *svadharma* (own dharma) is based on his stage and position in life, and on his *vāsanās* (inherent tendencies).

Dharma is ethics and religion combined. In general, it stands for all those ideals, purposes, influences, institutions, and ways of conduct that shape the character and evolution of a person, both as an individual and as a member of society. Dharma is the law of right living, the observance of which fulfills two objectives: happiness in life and liberation from all bondage.

Dhāraṇāt dharmam, "That which sustains is dharma" (*Mahābhārata*). *Mahābhārata*, which is a veritable encyclopedia of Indian wisdom, culture, and tradition, emphatically states, "Nobody has ever violated the principles of dharma without ultimately courting disaster." The text further states that *adharma* (unethical action) may carry a man to heights of power and prosperity for a time, but these gains are all temporary and eventually lead to his downfall.

5. What are some fundamental doctrines of Hinduism?

- The Vedas are the ultimate scriptural authority: The Vedas are divine sources of knowledge that reveal the eternal Truth.

- The Self is One, and is independent of the body, mind, and intellect: The human being is, in essence, neither the gross physical body, nor the subtle mind and intellect, but something beyond them. He is the *Ātman*, or the Self, the real Being behind the apparent individual.

- The doctrine of karma: The law of karma (the law of causality) states that we are the creators of our own destiny. Our present condition is due to our past conduct, and our future state will be based on our past and present thoughts and actions.

- The doctrine of reincarnation: The essential Self is, by nature, divine, pure, perfect, infinite, and free. It was never created and therefore will never die. However, the individual being (*jīvātman*) that one presently thinks oneself to be, due to ignorance, passes from body to body (reincarnates in different forms) in its onward journey to the realization of its perfection. For further study, see Chapter 2 of *The Holy Geeta* by Swami Chinmayananda.

- The existence of God as the creator, sustainer, and destroyer, with reference to the world of names and forms: God manifests Himself as the creative and preserving power of the whole universe, and unto Him, the universe returns. The entire phenomenal world rises, exists, dissolves, and again rises in Him. The three functions of creation, preservation, and dissolution are but different aspects of the same supreme Being. When we think of Him as the creator, we call Him *Brahmā*; when we think of Him as the preserver, we call Him *Vishṇu*; and when we think of Him as the (constructive) destroyer, we call Him *Shiva*.

6. Why does Hinduism say that the human being is, in essence, divine (*Ātman*)?

Hindus believe that the human being is essentially divine. Every human being—irrespective of caste, creed, color, gender, etc.—can attain the knowledge of this truth and make his life an expression of it. Perfection is not only open to all, but it is the very nature of all. It has only to be unfolded, revealed. There is no such thing as spiritual death.

The Vedas logically and conclusively prove that the essence of every human being is the one *Ātman* (Self). Logical thought reveals that the human being is not the body, the mind, or the intellect. He is something beyond these instruments, functioning through the body, the mind, and the intellect.

This is evident in our daily usage of such expressions as "my body," "my mind," etc. If I am the owner of the body, mind, etc., I must be other than the body, mind, etc.

Example: The statement, "This is my car" clearly shows that I am not the car, for it is an object of my perception.

When I apply the same thought process to "my body," "my mind," etc., I will conclude that the body, mind, etc. are my possessions, not my true being. By disidentifying with my instruments and related objects or persons, I will reach my essential Source, which cannot be denied or negated. For further study, see *Self Unfoldment* by Swami Chinmayananda.

7. What are the two doctrines of karma and reincarnation, and why do Hindus believe in them?

Hindus believe in the two doctrines of karma and reincarnation because these doctrines not only logically explain unusual occurrences, but also shed light on life's day-to-day events. Hindus do not consider life and death to be mutually exclusive, but as intertwined and inseparable, like two sides of the same coin. If there are disparities between two individuals at birth, and we see that there are, then the cause for these disparities must have preceded birth.

- Karma: The word *karma* means "action." In accordance with the cosmic laws of karma, each individual reaps the fruits of his actions, performed in this life or in former lives. This logically explains the disparities in creation, that is, between various individuals' environments and situations. No deed, small or great, good or bad, can be without an effect—this is the law of karma, the law of causality.

  Karma is not fate. Fate implies the helplessness of the human being to determine his own destiny. The law of karma states that the individual is the creator of his own destiny because his conscious choices in life determine his actions and the fruits thereof.

- Reincarnation: Hindus believe that the *jīva*, or the individual being, travels from life to life, acquiring bodies and environments best suited to exhaust his *vāsanās*, or innate tendencies that are expressed as desires, emotions, and actions. The exhaustion of *vāsanās* allows the *jīva* to reach his ultimate goal: complete freedom from the cycle of birth and death through the realization of his true nature as the Self, or *Brahman*.

8. What determines whether an act is a merit (*puṇya*) or a sin (*pāpa*)?

There are different types of karmas, or actions:

- *Nitya karma*s (daily duties)
- *Naimittika karma*s (special duties)
- *Kāmya karma*s (desire-born actions)
- *Nishiddha karma*s (wrongful actions)
- *Prāyaschitta karma*s (actions of penance to improve oneself)

Karmas are performed through three instruments:

- *Manas* (mind)
- *Vāk* (speech)
- *Kāyā* (body)

The results of karmas can be seen in these three categories:

- *Puṇya karma*s (meritorious, or *dhārmik*, actions, leading to good results)
- *Pāpa karma*s (wrong, or *adhārmik*, actions, leading to bad results)
- *Mishra karma*s (actions having mixed results)

Karmas by mind (thoughts): Noble thoughts about *bhakti* (devotion), *vairāgya* (dispassion), charity, spiritual evolution, etc. are mental *puṇya karma*s. Lustful thoughts pertaining to sense enjoyments, harming others, and disrespect for the scriptures, traditions, and dharma are mental *pāpa karma*s. An admixture of both types is known as *mishra karma*. In simple terms, Swami Chinmayananda explains *puṇya karma*s as "self-congratulatory acts" and *pāpa karma*s as "self-insulting acts."

Karmas by speech (words): Regularly reciting or reading the scriptures, chanting mantras and hymns, singing devotional songs, speaking truthful and noble words, offering others words of love and compassion, etc. are *puṇya karma*s performed by speech.

Words of disrespect for the scriptures, verbal abuse of the Lord and *mahātmā*s, engaging in lies or cruel, offensive, and unsympathetic talk, etc. are *pāpa* karmas of speech.

Karmas by body (actions): Bathing in holy waters, prostrating to your guru, the Lord, and saintly persons, performing worship (*pūjā*s), seeking the presence of holy beings, submitting to *tapas* (sacrifice and discipline), etc. are *puṇya karma*s of the body.

Immoral acts, causing injury to others, indulging in cruelty, associating with cruel persons, etc. are *pāpa karma*s of the body.

Troubling others while doing a good deed, misappropriation of another's wealth or property in the process of doing good work (e.g., building temples, giving charity), not giving proper remuneration for services rendered, etc., are all *mishra karma*s of the body.

Veda Vyāsa has said, *Paropakāra puṇyāya pāpāya parapīḍanam*, "Doing good to others at any of these three levels of body, speech, and mind is *puṇya*. Injuring others at any of these levels is *pāpa*." *Puṇya* is that which helps us evolve and *pāpa* is that by which we devolve or by which our progress stagnates. For further study, see *The Holy Geeta* by Swami Chinmayananda.

9. What is the Hindu concept of heaven and hell?

The Hindu concept of heaven and hell can be understood at different levels: physical and mental. Beyond these two levels, which are relative, is the absolute standpoint.

- At the physical level: The *Purāṇa*s expound on 14 different dimensions in God's creation, where heaven and hell exist as separate planes of existence. The realms of heaven and hell are described in detail in the scriptures and are planes where *jīva*s (individuals) exist in their subtle bodies.

  Heaven (*svarga*) is a plane where departed *jīva*s go to reap the fruits of their virtuous deeds and remain there until their merits are exhausted. In heaven, one knows no hunger, thirst, or disease, for there is no physical body. The enjoyments in heaven are more intense, subtle, and refined, but they still cannot give everlasting peace and bliss. The period for which the *jīva* stays in heaven depends upon the degree of his past meritorious deeds on Earth.

  The *Purāṇa*s speak of hell (*naraka*) as a plane where evildoers suffer for a period, in accordance with the fruits of their actions. It is presided over by Lord Yama, or the lord of death. The punishment meted out in hell is reformatory and educative, and is not remembered by the *jīva* upon rebirth.

  Hindus do not believe in a permanent state of heaven and hell; they are both transitory. An individual goes to heaven or hell depending on his past actions and, after exhausting his merits or demerits, comes back to Earth to strive for *moksha*, or liberation from the cycle of life and death. The planes of heaven and hell are thus intermediate stages in the individual's progress toward final liberation. For further study, see *Shrīmad Bhāgavatam*.

- At the mental level: From a subtler standpoint, heaven and hell are mental realms or fields of experience. When one's mind is filled with contentment, patience, compassion, forgiveness, and such values, one experiences a great degree of joy and lives in his own "heaven." When one's mind is filled with negativities, such as anger, greed, jealousy, etc., life is miserable and one is living in a self-created "hell." Thus, both heaven and hell are mental creations.

- From the absolute standpoint: On the absolute level, both heaven and hell are only projections of the mind, just as this waking world of names and forms is but a projection, born of ignorance, on *Brahman*. Heaven and hell are given relative reality only as long as the sense of individuality (ego) persists—as long as the individual has not realized his true Self. From the absolute standpoint of Oneness, there is nothing other than the one Reality. For further study, see *Māṇḍūkya Upanishad*.

10. What are the goals of human life according to Hindu ethics?

There are four goals of human life called *purushārtha*s:

- *Dharma*: righteous action
- *Artha*: acquisition of wealth and worldly possessions
- *Kāma*: fulfillment and enjoyment of desires
- *Moksha*: liberation from the cycle of birth and death

Dharma is listed as the first *purushārtha* because *artha* and *kāma* are to be obtained through methods sanctioned by the tenets of dharma. *Moksha* is the highest of the *purushārtha*s and is the ultimate goal of human life (see Question 63).

11. What are the four *āshrama*s, or stages, of an individual's life?

- *Brahmacharya*: the stage of living as a *brahmachārī*, a student or ardent disciple

- *Grihastha*: the stage of living as a householder
- *Vānaprastha*: the stage of living as a hermit
- *Sannyāsa*: the stage of living as a renunciate

Every human being is enjoined to go through all these stages in succession. Based on a 100-year life span, the average person would go through the stages as follows: 0-25 years—*brahmacharya*; 25-50 years—*grihastha*; 50-75 years—*vānaprastha*; 75-100 years—*sannyāsa*. By going through these stages, an individual discharges his familial and societal obligations, and finally liberates himself. It should be noted that there are guided or advanced spiritual seekers who bypass stages and go directly to *sannyāsa* because of their intense desire for liberation.

A person who has entered the stage of *sannyāsa* is called a *sannyāsī*. Lord Krishṇa defines *sannyāsa* in *Gītā* 18.2 as the renunciation of all *kāmya karma*s, or actions performed with a desire for the fruits thereof. Internal *sannyāsa* is an inner transformation, the renunciation of all desires. External *sannyāsa* refers to the renunciation of all external bonds and attachments for those seekers who want to, and are fit to, devote their lives to spiritual pursuit.

12. What is meant by "caste" in Hinduism?

The words "caste" and "caste system" are attributed to Hinduism, but are greatly misinterpreted and misunderstood concepts in society today. The caste system of today is the result of generations trying to preserve their knowledge, profession, social status, etc. by misusing and misinterpreting the scriptures for personal convenience. As the word is used today, *caste* is a categorization based on birth, profession, or social status. However, the scriptures do not condone this interpretation.

The Hindu scriptures expound on the three *guṇa*s (inner dispositions): *sattva* (expressed as creativity, inspiration, mental quietude, etc.), *rajas* (expressed as restlessness, dynamism, mental agitation, etc.), and *tamas* (expressed as laziness, negligence, dullness, etc.). An individual's personality is comprised of changing permutations of these three *guṇa*s, and expresses at the mental level as thoughts and at the physical level as actions.

In *Shrīmad Bhagavad Gītā*, Lord Krishṇa states that a person's disposition is of his own making, the result of his own choices and actions. *Gītā* uses the term *varṇa*, or color, to describe an individual's personality and, based on the three *guṇa*s, categorizes humanity into four *varṇa*s or castes:

- *Brāhmaṇa*s (Brahmins): the thinkers, who have a preponderance of *sāttvik* qualities on a *rājasik* base, whose duty it is to lead society along the righteous path and be role models in secular and spiritual matters

- *Kshatriya*s: the leaders or warriors, with a preponderance of *rājasik* qualities on a *sāttvik* base, whose duty it is to protect and nurture society

- *Vaishya*s: the businessmen or financiers, with a preponderance of *rājasik* qualities on a *tāmasik* base, whose duty it is to fulfill society's economic needs

- *Shūdra*s: the laborers, with a preponderance of *tāmasik* qualities on a *rājasik* base, whose duty it is to contribute labor for society's progress and well-being

Gītā teaches that one's *varṇa* is not based on one's birth, lineage, or profession, and therefore, no one can be deemed superior or inferior in society based on these superficial factors. One's *varṇa* is determined by which *guṇa*s one chooses to develop and express. At any given time, each individual falls primarily into one of the four *varṇa*s, based on his predominant tendencies. However, there is always room for change and growth. The highest goal is to recognize the one Spirit behind all the veils of *varṇa*. For further study, see *The Holy Geeta* by Swami Chinmayananda.

13. What is the spiritual significance of joining one's palms in *namaskāra* or *namaste*?

The traditional Hindu greeting of *namaskāra* or *namaste* is for one and all, and is done by reverently joining the palms at the chest and humbly bowing the head. *Namaskāra* is a form of prostration and salutation, and has profound spiritual significance.

In Sanskrit, *namaḥ* + *te* = *namaste*. It means, "I bow to you; my prostrations and salutations to you." *Namaḥ* can also be literally interpreted as *na mama*, meaning, "not mine." The purpose of saying *namaste* is thus to negate one's ego (sense of separateness) and recognize the Divine in every person we greet, for the life force, Self, or Lord in me, is the same in all. The joining of the palms depicts this sense of Oneness. When we know this significance, our greeting paves the way for a deeper, divine communion, complete with love and respect.

14. What is the spiritual significance of the marks on the forehead of *bindi*, *tilak*, and *tripuṇḍra*?

The *bindi*, *tilak*, and *tripuṇḍra* are traditionally applied on the forehead with *kumkum* (vermilion powder), *chandan* (sandalwood paste), or *bhasma* (sacred ash).

The *bindi* or *tilak* (dot or vertical line applied between the eyebrows) symbolizes the third eye of wisdom or enlightenment, which opens when the spiritual seeker has purified his mind, made it single-pointed, and gone beyond relative existence to merge into pure Consciousness.

The *tripuṇḍra* (three horizontal lines applied across the forehead) symbolizes various triads that the seeker has to transcend: the syllables of Om (or A-U-M), which represent the planes of waking, dream, and deep sleep; the *guṇa*s of *sattva*, *rajas*, and *tamas*; the instruments of gross body, subtle body, and causal body; the experiencer, experience, and experienced; etc. The wearing of the *bindi*, *tilak*, or *tripuṇḍra* thus serves as a constant reminder to the seeker of his ultimate goal of Self-realization.

PART TWO

SCRIPTURES

PART TWO: SCRIPTURES

15. Describe the two main categories of Hindu scriptures: *shruti* and *smriti*.

The sacred books of the Hindus fall under two broad categories: *shruti* and *smriti*. Hindus believe that the *shruti*s are God-revealed and eternal, and the *smriti*s are man-made, passed down through generations, according to the needs of the time. The *shruti*s deal with fundamental principles that hold true for all time, while the *smriti*s deal with the practical application of those eternal principles according to changing times. In fact, there is a *shruti* content in every religion.

The word *shruti*, "that which is heard," refers to the Vedas. The word *smriti*, "that which is remembered," refers to the codes of conduct, set forth in texts like *Manu Smriti*, by which human beings should live.

16. What does *veda* mean?

The word *veda* comes from the root *vid*, "to know." *Veda* literally means "the book of knowledge." It is a compendium containing sacred and secular knowledge.

17. How many Vedas are there, what do they deal with, and what sections do they consist of?

Veda is one book of knowledge divided into four portions, but these portions are commonly referred to as the four Vedas, namely:

- *Rig Veda*: hymns of praise; believed to be the oldest book known to humanity and one of the most precious collections of knowledge

- *Yajur Veda*: special directions and formulas for the preparation and performance of rituals and ceremonies

- *Sāma Veda*: melodies and songs, with precise intonations and modulations, to be chanted at rituals; the most voluminous of the four Vedas

- *Atharva Veda*: mystical formulas; Tantric and other forms of esoteric knowledge, which paved the way for modern science in India

Each *Veda* consists of three sections, namely:

- *Saṁhitās*: the mantra portion, consisting of hymns of praise for Vedic deities

- *Brāhmaṇas*: the ritualistic portion, dealing with the methodology of performing Vedic rituals

- *Āraṇyakas*: the contemplative portion, including the Upanishads

18. What are the *Upa-vedas*, how many are there, and what do they deal with?

The *Upa-vedas*, or *Veda-upāṅgas*, are writings subordinate to the Vedas. They are four in number, one attached to each of the four Vedas:

- In *Rig Veda*: *Āyurveda*, the science of medicine and health

- In *Yajur Veda*: *Dhanur Veda*, military science

- In *Sāma Veda*: *Gandharva Veda*, the art and science of music

- In *Atharva Veda*: *Sthāpatya Veda*, the science of mechanics and construction

19. What are the *Vedāṅgas*?

There are six *Vedāṅgas* that are the additional limbs of the Vedas:

- *Chhandas*: prosody (science of poetic meters)
- *Jyotisha*: astronomy and astrology
- *Kalpa*: construction and design of religious sites
- *Nirukta*: Vedic etymology
- *Shikshā*: phonetics
- *Vyākaraṇa*: grammar

20. What are the schools of Hindu philosophy?

There are six *darshanas*, or schools, of Hindu philosophy, each independent of the other, but each accepting the Vedas as the scriptural authority:

- *Nyāya* of Sage Gautama: deals with the Hindu system of logic
- *Vaisheshika* of Sage Kannāda: deals with the atomic theory and structure of the universe
- *Sānkhya* of Sage Kapila: deals with the relationship between Nature and Spirit as the cause of the world
- *Yoga* of Sage Patanjali: deals with gaining mastery over oneself through the transformation of one's inner equipment
- *Mīmāṁsā* of Sage Jaimini: deals with the procedure and practice of rituals; a treatise on *Karma Kāṇḍa*; also known as *Pūrva Mīmāṁsā*
- *Vedānta* of Sage Krishṇa Dvaipāyana Bādarāyaṇa Vyāsa (Sage Veda Vyāsa): deals with the philosophical and theological views in the Upanishads; also known as *Uttara Mīmāṁsā*

21. What does *Vedānta* mean?

The term *Vedānta* means:

- *Veda* + *anta*, "the end of the Vedas," which literally means the concluding portion of the Vedas, but refers to the end goal indicated by the Vedas: *Brahman*

- *Vede siddhyati siddhānta iti vedānta*, "the philosophical conclusions arrived at, by, and in the Vedas"

22. Does Vedantic philosophy include different schools of thought? If so, what are they?

The Hindu seers (*rishi*s) were never satisfied unless they discussed every question to its logical and irrefutable conclusion, and this led to different schools of philosophical thought.

There were six Vedantic schools of thought that developed over time, all claiming to be based on Upanishadic teachings. They are (in chronological order, from the earliest):

- *Advaita* of Ādi Shaṅkarāchārya
- *Vishishṭādvaita* (*Vishishṭa Advaita*) of Rāmānujāchārya
- *Dvaita* of Madhvāchārya
- *Shuddhādvaita* (*Shuddha Advaita*) of Vallabhāchārya
- *Dvaitādvaita* (*Dvaita Advaita*) of Nimbārkāchārya
- *Achintyabhedābheda* (*Achintya-bheda-abheda*) of Jīva Gosvāmin

23. How do we reconcile the different schools of philosophy and different approaches to the Truth?

The apparently divergent scriptures have been given by different teachers at different periods of time to suit different types of students. Amid this diversity, one finds that although the paths are different, the goal is the same. Each teacher vehemently emphasizes a path that is best suited for the benefit of his disciples. A true student is able to see through these apparent differences and remain firm on his own path.

Different schools of philosophy are merely different notions about, and interpretations of, the same subject. Differences will exist when teachers and scriptures are trying to describe the indescribable. *Amrita-bindu Upanishad* says, *Gavām aneka-varṇānām, kshīrasya-api-eka-varṇatā, kshīravat pashyate jñānam, liṅginastu gavām yathā*: "Cows are of different colors. But the milk from all the cows is the same color—white. So too, the intelligent one should regard knowledge as the milk and the sources of such knowledge as the cows."

Scriptures may differ in words and interpretations, but all speak of and indicate the same Truth. The milk is of the main concern for the cowherd; so too, knowledge (not its source) should be the main concern for the sincere seeker.

24. What are the three main scriptural sources for a Vedantin?

Prasthāna-traya refers to the three sources of scriptural authority for a Vedantin. These are:

- Upanishads
- *Brahma Sūtras*
- *Shrīmad Bhagavad Gītā*

These are the three accepted sources from which the different schools of Vedanta derive their authority. Of the *prasthāna-traya*, the *Brahma Sūtras* are *nyāya pramāṇa* (means of knowledge with an emphasis on logic); the *Bhagavad Gītā* is *smriti pramāṇa* (means of knowledge with an emphasis on the *smritis*); and the Upanishads are *shruti pramāṇa* (means of knowledge with an emphasis on the *shrutis*).

25. What are the Upanishads?

The Upanishads are the first source of scriptural authority in the *prasthāna-traya*. The Upanishads generally form the end portion of the *Āraṇyakas* of the Vedas, and therefore the philosophy described therein is called Vedanta, which means "the end of the Vedas." It is important not to take this definition literally, as Upanishads also appear in other sections of the Vedas and are distinguished as such through their subject matter: the supreme Reality. The Upanishads are texts that deal with the highest knowledge—the knowledge of the pure Self—and are thus the ultimate teaching, the end goal indicated by the Vedas.

The Upanishads contain the essence of Vedic teachings. They are the foundation on which most of the later philosophies of India rest. There is no important form of spiritual thought originating in India that has not been derived from the Upanishads.

The word *Upanishad* consists of three syllables: *upa-ni-shad*, meaning, "near-below-sit." This meaning denotes the flow of knowledge from the higher to the lower level, from the guru to the *shishya* (disciple). The word also reflects the reverential attitude of the *shishya*, who physically sits below the level of the guru, near his feet. For further study, see Ādi Shaṅkarāchārya's *Vivekachūḍāmaṇi* and introduction to *Kaṭha Upanishad*.

26. How many Upanishads are there?

There are 1,179 Upanishads, as follows:

- 21 in *Rig Veda*
- 108 in *Yajur Veda*
- 1,000 in *Sāma Veda*
- 50 in *Atharva Veda*

Tradition considers 108 Upanishads (see Appendix) as important and authoritative. Of these 108, ten are considered as the major Upanishads:

Aitareya	*Kena*
Brihadāraṇyaka	*Māṇḍūkya*
Chhāndogya	*Muṇḍaka*
Īshāvāsya	*Prashna*
Kaṭha	*Taittirīya*

27. What are the great declarations, or *mahāvākyas*, and where are they found in the Vedas?

The quintessence of Vedanta is found in "great declarations" called *mahāvākyas*. These are numerous and appear throughout the Vedas in different places. There are four popularly known *mahāvākyas*, culled from four Upanishads, one from each of the four Vedas.

Though every *mahāvākya* is complete by itself and has the potential to grant liberation to a fit aspirant, a common, sequential storyline to connect the teachings in the four *mahāvākyas* and provide a roadmap for *sādhanā*, is given as follows:

- *Prajñānam Brahma*: "Consciousness is Brahman." (*Aitareya Upanishad, Rig Veda*)

This first *mahāvākya* is the *lakshaṇa vākya* (statement of definition), for it gives a definition of Truth. It declares that Consciousness, the spiritual core that enlivens each of us, is the same all-pervading Consciousness in all beings and things.

- *Tat Tvam Asi*: "That Thou Art." (*Chhāndogya Upanishad, Sāma Veda*)

The disciple, after reflecting on the guru's teachings, still has doubts. In the second *mahāvākya*, the *upadesha vākya* (statement of instruction), the guru tells the disciple that he (the disciple) is verily the supreme *Brahman* and not the limited personality he imagines himself to be.

Thus, the Truth the disciple is seeking is none other than his own Self and is to be found within. This state of Consciousness is to be realized here and now through Self-inquiry.

- *Aham Brahma Asmi*: "I am Brahman." (*Brihadāraṇyaka Upanishad, Yajur Veda*)

Through meditation, after overcoming his habitual thinking of the Truth as something other than himself, the student comes back to the master filled with his intimate and direct experience of the Truth. His experience is of the nature of this *mahāvākya*, which is the *anubhava vākya* (statement of experience).

- *Ayam Ātmā Brahma*: "This Self is Brahman." (*Māṇḍūkya Upanishad, Atharva Veda*)

Once the disciple is established in his real nature, the guru advises him to constantly revel and abide in the Self. The nature of his abidance is expressed by this *mahāvākya*, which is the *anusandhāna vākya* (statement of constant practice).

28. What are *sūtras*?

Sūtras are systematic treatises in the form of aphorisms. They act as pointers and memory aids for intensive discussions on any topic. *Padma Purāṇa* gives the following requirements for the creation of a *sūtra*:

- Should be concise to facilitate memorization
- Should hold no ambiguity
- Should give the essence of various viewpoints on a topic, covering all aspects of the question
- Should use only words that are absolutely necessary, relevant, and meaningful
- Should be capable of being understood from all perspectives
- Should not be repetitious
- Should not have any logical fallacies

Examples: The *Brahma Sūtras* of Veda Vyāsa, the *Yoga Sūtras* of Patanjali, and the *Bhakti Sūtras* of Sage Nārada

29. What are the *Brahma Sūtras*?

The *Brahma Sūtras*, also known as *Shārīrika Sūtras*, are the second source of scriptural authority in the *prasthāna-traya*. The *Brahma Sūtras* are a compendium of 555 aphorisms by Sage Veda Vyāsa. The *sūtras* present, in a concentrated form, the entire philosophy of the Upanishads. In this textbook for postgraduate Vedantic studies, Sage Vyāsa leads the student into the inquiry of the nature of the supreme Reality, the relationship between the human being and the supreme Reality, the ultimate fulfillment of human birth and existence, and the means to realize this fulfillment.

30. What is *Shrīmad Bhagavad Gītā*?

Shrīmad Bhagavad Gītā is the third source of scriptural authority in the *prasthāna-traya*. *Bhagavad Gītā*, or the "Lord's Song," written by Sage Veda Vyāsa, is traditionally comprised of 700 *shloka*s, or verses (1 said by Dhritarāshṭra, 41 said by Sanjaya, 84 said by Arjuna, and 574 said by Lord Krishṇa).

There is also a widely accepted version of *Gītā* that contains 701 verses. The spiritual teacher, Shrī Madhusūdana Sarasvatī, who also authored *Gītā Dhyānam* and the concluding colophon at the end of each *Gītā* chapter, added a question to open Chapter 13. The 18 chapters of *Gītā* are found in *Mahābhārata*: *Bhīshma Parva* 25-42.

Shrīmad Bhagavad Gītā is the most popular, profound, and poetic philosophical composition in Sanskrit literature. It is said to be perhaps the only philosophical song of its kind existing in any known language. It is a text that conveys sublime spiritual teachings and the art of living. If the hold that a specific work has on the mind of a human being is any indication of its importance, then *Shrīmad Bhagavad Gītā* is the most influential work in Indian thought. It is the only philosophical treatise in the world that was delivered on a battlefield and, as such, also has great allegorical significance. Its teachings are timeless; they are applicable at a universal level and address humanity everywhere, at all times, in all aspects.

31. What are the *Purāṇa*s and how many are there?

There are 18 *Purāṇa*s and they generally deal with these five topics:

- *Sarga*: primary creation or cosmogony
- *Pratisarga*: secondary creation, sustenance, destruction, and re-creation of worlds, including chronology
- *Vaṁsha*: genealogy of deities and patriarchs

- *Manvantara*: reigns of the different Manus

- *Vaṁshānucharita*: history of the solar and lunar dynasties, and their descendants

The 18 *Mahā-purāṇa*s are divided into three categories of six:

- Brāhma Purāṇas: *Brahma*, *Brahmāṇḍa*, *Brahma-vaivarta*, *Bhavishya*, *Mārkaṇḍeya*, *Vāmana*

- Vaishṇava Purāṇas: *Vishṇu*, *Bhāgavata*, *Garuḍa*, *Nāradīya*, *Padma*, *Varāha*

- Shaiva Purāṇas: *Shiva* (*Vāyu*), *Agni*, *Kūrma*, *Liṅga*, *Matsya*, *Skanda*

In addition to these 18 *Purāṇa*s, there are 46 *Upa-purāṇa*s. Of the 46 *Upa-purāṇa*s, 18 are prominent:

Bhārgava	*Kalika*	*Sanat Kumāra*
Brihannāradīya	*Kapila*	*Shiva-rahasya*
Devī Bhāgavata	*Nandi*	*Sūrya*
Durvāsa	*Narasiṁha*	*Vāmana*
Gaṇesha	*Parāshara*	*Varuṇa*
Haṁsa	*Sāmba*	*Vāsishṭha*

32. What are the two major historical epics in Hinduism?

Rāmāyaṇa and *Mahābhārata* are the two *Itihāsa*s, or historical sagas, that serve as an inspiration for humanity and exemplify the realization of the four *purushārtha*s: dharma (righteous and dutiful living), *artha* (wealth), *kāma* (desire fulfillment), and *moksha* (liberation).

- *Rāmāyaṇa* literally means "the abode of Rāma" and it is the smaller of the two works. The epic mirrors the highest ideals of Hindu tradition, culture, and civilization. The story, which took place in *Tretā Yuga* (one of the four ages of the world; see Question 36), centers on Rāma, the prince of Ayodhyā and the incarnation of Lord Vishṇu, and his wife Sītā, the incarnation of Mother Lakshmī. *Rāmāyaṇa* sings the Lord's glories and instructs humanity on how to lead a fulfilling life and attain the four *purushārthas*. The epic is profound and timeless in its popularity, and teaches, with the use of symbolism, how an individual can evolve to greatness and perfection.

  Sage Vālmīki's *Rāmāyaṇa* has been translated into most Indian languages, as well as several foreign languages, including Russian. It consists of 24,000 stanzas in seven cantos, and depicts Rāma as the ideal king, son, brother, friend, and husband. In Bharata, Lakshmaṇa, and Shatrughna, we see exemplified the ideal brothers. In Sītā, we have the purest flower of Indian womanhood, who is devoted to her Lord in thought, word, and deed.

  Rāmāyaṇa is an ideal textbook of morals and values that inspires nobler dimensions of character and conduct. Other noteworthy and famous versions of *Rāmāyaṇa* include Sage Veda Vyāsa's *Adhyātma Rāmāyaṇa*, Goswāmī Tulasīdāsa's *Shrī Rāmacharitamānasa* (*Tulasī Rāmāyaṇa*), and Kambar's *Kamba Rāmāyaṇa*.

- *Mahābhārata* is an epic that is more than eight times the size of Homer's *Iliad* and *Odyssey* combined, and in philosophical content is unparalleled to any other literary work in the world. This grand book of knowledge contains more than 100,000 stanzas in 18 chapters and is the work of the renowned Sage Veda Vyāsa.

  The underlying theme of *Mahābhārata* is *yato dharma tato jayaḥ*, "where there is dharma, there is victory," indicating the ultimate triumph of good over evil and the establishment of righteousness.

The story unfolds toward the end of *Dvāpara Yuga*, and describes the genealogy and events leading up to, and after, the familial war between royal cousins.

The story is used as a vehicle to convey eternal philosophical truths of the highest order. It is said, "That which is in *Mahābhārata* can be seen elsewhere, but that which is not therein cannot be seen anywhere else." This gives an idea of the comprehensiveness of subjects in the epic, which is full of lofty instructions on all aspects of human life and endeavor—an inspiring saga of India's past glory, portraying all that is great and noble in humanity.

The guiding spirit throughout the epic is the divine figure of Lord Krishṇa, who brings the pure and the righteous to Himself, and who destroys evil and evildoers. *Shrīmad Bhagavad Gītā* or the "Lord's Song," is part of *Mahābhārata.*

33. What is *Shrīmad Bhāgavatam*?

The Sanskrit term *Bhāgavata* means "pertaining to the Lord": He who has (the six) glories. *Shrīmad Bhāgavata Purāṇa*, or *Shrīmad Bhāgavatam*, is commonly referred to as *Bhāgavata*, or *Bhāgavatam*, and it is undoubtedly the most voluminous and popular of the *Purāṇa*s.

This devotional text portrays the sagas of Lord Vishṇu's various *avatāra*s (incarnations), focusing on the life of Lord Krishṇa. *Shrīmad Bhāgavatam* remains unrivaled in its stories, expressions, and teachings on devotion, knowledge, and action, all dedicated to the Divine.

34. What is *Yoga Vāsishṭha*?

Yoga Vāsishṭha is a book of 36,000 verses from the pen of the celebrated Sage Vālmīki, the author of *Rāmāyaṇa*. Sage Vasishṭha's spiritual teachings and advice to Shrī Rāma comprise the subject matter of this highly philosophical treatise. The method employed by Sage

Vasishṭha is unique, as he conveys profound philosophical truths to Shrī Rāma through the narration of innumerable stories.

35. What are the *Dharma Shāstras*, how many are there, and who wrote them?

The *Dharma Shāstra*s are works by various sages. They are social laws that include the codes of conduct to be observed by individuals throughout their lives.

Manu's *Dharma Shāstra*, also known as *Manu Smriti*, is the fundamental *dharma shāstra* that is applicable to the entire *manvantara* (time period until the appearance of the next Manu; see Question 36). *Manu Smriti* forms the basis of Hindu law.

Additionally, there are 18 specific *Dharma Shāstra*s that are applicable in different periods of time. The 18 *Dharma Shāstra*s are named after their authors:

Āpastamba	*Bharadvāja*	*Daksha*
Devala	*Samakha*	*Vāsishṭha*
Gautama	*Saṁvarta*	*Vishṇu*
Harita	*Shatānīka*	*Vyāsa*
Likhita	*Shaṭotraya*	*Yājñavalkya*
Parāshara	*Shaunaka*	*Yama*

36. Who is Manu and what is a *manvantara*, or the Hindu calculation of time?

Antara means "space" or "duration between." Therefore, a *manvantara* is the period of time or duration that a Manu (the archetypal human being) rules the entire creation. Hindus calculated time based on *manvantaras*. Western scientists and archaeologists later discovered that these *manvantaras* are based on accurate astronomical calculations.

One *manvantara* is calculated as follows:

- 360 human years make one *divya varsha* (celestial year)
- 4,800 *divya varshas* make one *Satya Yuga*, or *Krita Yuga*
- 3,600 *divya varshas* make one *Tretā Yuga*
- 2,400 *divya varshas* make one *Dvāpara Yuga*
- 1,200 *divya varshas* make one *Kali Yuga*

All the *yugas* together total 12,000 *divya varshas*, and this one cycle of all the *yugas* makes one *mahā-yuga* or *chatur-yuga*. One *manvantara* = 71 *mahā-yugas*, or 306,720,000 human years. One *kalpa*, or cycle of creation, preservation, and destruction = 14 *manvantaras*. Thus, the cycle of time continues.

At the beginning of each *manvantara*, a Manu appears and codifies all ethical and social regulations to be followed during the *manvantara*. The Manu whose code is currently being followed is Vaivasvata Manu, who is the seventh in the line of the cycle of 14 Manus. The six Manus who preceded Vaivasvata Manu were: Svāyambhuva, Svārochisha, Uttama, Tāmasa, Raivata, and Chākshusha. The seven who will follow Vaivasvata Manu are: Sāvarṇi, Daksha-sāvarṇi, Brahma-sāvarṇi, Dharma-sāvarṇi, Rudra-sāvarṇi, Deva-sāvarṇi, and Indra-sāvarṇi.

37. Is there any special significance of the number 18 in the Hindu scriptures?

Yes. Aside from the fact that there are 18 *Purāṇas*, 18 major *Upa-purāṇas*, and 18 *Dharma Shāstras,* the significance of the number 18 is best illustrated in *Mahābhārata*, which is divided into 18 *parvas*, or sections. The Mahābhārata War was fought with 18 army divisions: 11 on the Kaurava side and 7 on the Pāṇḍava side. The war lasted 18 days. Finally, it is said that only 18 persons survived the war. The treatise *Shrīmad Bhagavad Gītā* is a part of *Mahābhārata* and has 18 chapters. In *Gītā*, Lord Krishṇa describes the ideal man in 18 verses at the end of Chapter 2, in which he lists the 18 traits that constitute the man of steady wisdom.

The theme of all scriptures of all religions in the world is the same: the victory of the higher Self over the lower self, of righteousness over unrighteousness, of good over evil, of dharma over *adharma*. Veda Vyāsa originally titled *Mahābhārata* as *Jaya* (victory). The word *jaya* is in the opening stanzas of both, *Mahābhārata* and *Gītā*.

In Sanskrit numerology, the Katapayadi System, each letter has a formula-based, numerical value. The numerical value of the word *jaya* is 18. To stress the importance of the word *jaya*, the number 18 is given a prominent place not only in *Mahābhārata*, but also throughout various Hindu scriptures. The number 18 is thus repeatedly used as an auspicious reminder to be alert in our constant battle for inner, spiritual victory.

PART THREE

MANTRAS AND WORSHIP

PART THREE: MANTRAS AND WORSHIP

38. What does *Om* mean?

Om is the all-encompassing, sacred symbol that represents the infinite, indefinable *Brahman*, the Reality indicated by the Vedas, the all-pervading substratum of this universe. Om is *praṇava*, or God as the primal sound. It is solemnly chanted at the commencement of all prayers and rituals, and is an aid to concentration and contemplation.

Om is comprised of three syllables, *a-u-m*, which represent our three states of experience, namely, waking, dream, and deep sleep. Collectively, Om represents the fourth state, the superconscious state known as *Turīya*. Om is a vast and subtle subject; for further study, see *Māṇḍūkya Upanishad*.

39. What is a mantra?

A mantra is a sacred word or words recited and contemplated upon during worship. *Mananāt trāyate iti mantraḥ*: "That (word or phrase) which leads us to the highest Goal through reflection upon it is called a mantra."

40. What is the *Gāyatrī Mantra*?

Om bhūr bhuvaḥ suvaḥ
Tat savitur vareṇyam
Bhargo devasya dhīmahi
Dhiyo yo naḥ prachodayāt

"We meditate on Om, the supreme Reality that pervades earth, interspace, and the heavens, that is the worshipful and adored Lord Sun, who shines as the light of Consciousness in our intellects. Burn away our ignorance and illumine our intellects [with the wisdom of the highest Truth]."

The *Gāyatrī Mantra* (*Rig Veda* 3.62.10) is one of the most ancient and divine hymns, and is the quintessence of the Vedas and Hindu culture. The mantra, originally revealed in meditation to Rishi Vishvāmitra, is a treasure of knowledge in both spiritual and secular fields, for it grants the aspirant cosmic energy, acute intelligence, subtle discrimination, creative vision, healing powers, and, ultimately, Self-realization.

The word *gāyatrī* literally means *gāyantam trāyate iti gāyatrī*, "that [mantra] which protects the one who sings or chants it." *Trāyate* also means "that which takes one across the ocean of transmigration or saves one from the cycle of birth and death." Chanting the *Gāyatrī Mantra* invokes divinity in a person and blesses him with spiritual illumination. This universal prayer for ultimate enlightenment is not chanted for material gain.

In some ancient texts, the *Gāyatrī Mantra* is also referred to as *Sāvitrī-Gāyatrī*, indicating that it is an invocation to the Lord in the form of the sun: Lord Sun. Lord Sun represents the giver of Light (Knowledge), the illuminator of all experiences, *Ātman*. As pure Consciousness, Lord Sun is the core of our being, around which all our matter envelopments revolve, just as the entire solar system revolves around the sun with mathematical precision. Just as there would be no life on Earth without the sun, so too, we would be mere inert matter without the *Ātman*.

The *Gāyatrī Mantra* is central to the teachings of yoga, Vedanta, *Āyurveda*, and Vedic astrology. In yoga, it transforms the *yogī* by stimulating his *kuṇḍalinī shakti*. To the Vedantin, it grants Self-knowledge. To the practitioner of *Āyurveda*, the mantra bestows the power of the cosmic *prāṇa*, which is born of the sun. For the *jyotisha*, or astrologer, it grants the knowledge of the movements of the heavenly bodies ruled by the cosmic sun.

The Vedic meter in which this powerful mantra is composed has also come to be called *Gāyatrī*. The *Gāyatrī* meter consists of three lines of eight syllables each.

41. Do Hindus worship idols or images?

Hindus do not worship idols or images per se, but rather the ideals that the idols or images represent. Human beings, with their finite instruments of knowledge, cannot conceive of the formless Infinite, so they use images as aids to concentration. Mahatma Gandhi said, "An idol does not excite any feeling of veneration in me. But I think that idol worship is part of human nature. We hanker after symbolism. Why should one be more composed in a church than elsewhere? Images are an aid to worship. No Hindu considers an image to be God."

Examples of symbolism in Hinduism: Lord Gaṇesha's elephant ears represent his ability of selective hearing—to listen to all that is auspicious and worthwhile, and to ignore the rest. Lord Shiva's snakes represent his victory over fear, death, and ego. Lord Krishṇa's blue color symbolizes infinity, like the infinitude of the blue sky. For further study, see *Symbolism in Hinduism* by Swami Chinmayananda.

The names and forms of God may be many, but God is One. Example: There are many types of golden ornaments, but the essence of all the ornaments is gold. So too, there are many names and forms in the universe, but the essence of all names and forms is One (God).

Devotion, Swami Chinmayananda says, is not "falling in love;" it is "rising in love." Most people need to associate a specific name and form with God because this makes it easier for them to develop a relationship with God. Which name and form each person chooses as his *ishṭa deva*, or Lord of his heart, is based on his personal attraction toward that name and form.

42. Can one worship God without the use of images?

Yes, one could worship God as *nirguṇa* and *nirākāra* (without qualities and without form). But it is easier to concentrate on God as *saguṇa* (with form) through a symbol. The Upanishads say that the formless *Brahman* has been assigned forms only for the convenience of the aspirant, as it is not possible for most people to concentrate on that which is formless.

43. Do Hindus worship cows and the natural elements?

Hindus revere cows because they regard all of creation as sacred—whether conscious or inert, whether animal or plant. It is not that Hindus worship cows as deities. Hindus honor cows in gratitude for their generosity, value, and gentleness. The cow is looked upon as a mother, who contributes unconditionally, in so many ways, to the daily sustenance of the human being.

Vedic hymns do address the natural elements, but the seeker is told to focus on the elements' underlying powers and not merely their physical aspects. Each element has *ādhibhautik* (physical), *ādhidaivik* (celestial), and *ādhyātmik* (spiritual) significance. Example: *Agni* signifies fire on the physical plane, purity on the celestial plane, and Light, or God, on the spiritual plane.

44. Who make up the Hindu Trinity?

The Hindu Trinity consists of Brahmā, the Creator (note the distinctions between Brahmā, *Brahman*, and *brāhmaṇa*); Vishṇu, the Sustainer; and Shiva, the Destroyer. The three represent the different aspects of the one *Brahman*, supreme Reality, or God.

It should be noted that the formless One has been assigned such forms only for the convenience of the seeker (*sādhakānām hitārthāya brahmaṇo rūpa-kalpanā*), whose finite equipment does not allow him to comprehend the infinite, formless One in its entirety.

45. What is meant by *avatāra*, or incarnation of God?

The Sanskrit term *avataraṇa* means "coming down" and denotes the manifestation of the Supreme in any form. Lord Krishṇa says in *Shrīmad Bhagavad Gītā* (4.7-4.8):

Yadā yadā hi dharmasya glānir bhavati bhārata
Abhyuthānam adharmasya tad ātmānam srijāmyaham
Paritrāṇāya sādhūnām vināshāya cha dushkritām
Dharma saṁsthāpanārthāya sambhavāmi yuge yuge

"Whenever righteousness declines and unrighteousness increases, I manifest Myself. I am born from age to age for the protection of the good, for the destruction of evil and evildoers, and the re-establishment of dharma in the world."

Thus, the *avatāra*, which is the incarnation of God in a form—to redeem humanity from spiritual degradation and restore dharma in society—postulates the ultimate victory and supremacy of the Divine.

46. Are all *avatāras* alike, or is there a difference between one *avatāra* and another?

Not all *avatāras* are alike. The Lord is ever complete, but His *avatāras* differ in manifestation, depending on the purpose of the incarnation, the requirements of the time, and the intensity of the circumstances. Based on this, *avatāras* are categorized as follows:

- *Nitya Avatāra*: The Lord is ever present in the world in the form of saints and sages. Saint Rāmdās said, "Those who work for the establishment of dharma are none other than *Īshvara* Himself."

- *Aṁsha Avatāra*: The Lord manifests with only a part of His potency in order to accomplish a particular goal. Example: *Matsya* (fish) *Avatāra*, *Varāha* (boar) *Avatāra*, *Vāmana* (dwarf) *Avatāra*, etc.

- *Āvesha Avatāra*: The Lord suddenly manifests in a situation where a devotee is in need. Example: *Narasiṁha Avatāra*, for His devotee Prahlāda.

- *Pūrṇa Avatāra*: The Lord manifests in His full potency and splendor (with all His 16 *kalās*, or attributes). Shrī Krishṇa is a *pūrṇa avatāra*.

47. What are the *avatāras* of Lord Vishṇu?

There have been various *avatāras* of Lord Vishṇu; however, it is not possible to give an exact number. This is largely due to the fact that whenever we see a great personality of superhuman strength (physical, mental, intellectual, or spiritual) establishing dharma and achieving great feats, we attribute it to divinity. *Shrīmad Bhāgavatam* states that even though there are countless *avatāras*, there are 24 *avatāras* that are significant. The ten renowned manifestations of Lord Vishṇu are:

Matsya (fish)	Parashurāma
Kūrma (tortoise)	Rāma
Varāha (boar)	Krishṇa
Narasiṁha (man-lion)	Buddha (or Balarāma)
Vāmana (dwarf)	Kalki

For further study, see *Shrīmad Bhāgavatam*.

PART FOUR

THE MEANS AND THE GOAL

PART FOUR: THE MEANS AND THE GOAL

48. What are the three dispositions (*guṇas*) of Nature?

- *Sattva* (*sattva-guṇa*): good, pious, noble, tranquil
- *Rajas* (*rajoguṇa*): passionate, agitated, authoritative, assertive
- *Tamas* (*tamoguṇa*): dull, inactive, sleepy, ignorant

These dispositions of Nature are seen at the macrocosmic and microcosmic levels of existence. On the microcosmic level, the sum total of all three qualities is always a constant; when one *guṇa* rises, the others decline. A person's personality or mood at any given time is determined by the preponderance of any one *guṇa*.

49. What are the five subtle elements, or *tan-mātras*?

The five subtle elements, before grossification, are known as the *tan-mātras*: space, air, fire, water, and earth. Each *tan-mātra* is comprised of the three *guṇas*: *sattva*, *rajas*, and *tamas*. Each *tan-mātra* has a total aspect and an individual aspect.

- The total *sāttvik* aspects of the five *tan-mātras* combine to form the *antaḥ-karaṇa*, or inner instrument: *manas*, *buddhi*, *chitta*, and *ahaṁkāra* (see Question 53).

  The individual *sāttvik* aspects of the five *tan-mātras* produce the *jñāna-indriyas*, or sense organs of perception: ears (from space), skin (from air), eyes (from fire), tongue (from water), and nose (from earth).

- The total *rājasik* aspects of the five *tan-mātras* combine to form the five *prāṇas*: *prāṇa*, *apāna*, *vyāna*, *udāna*, and *samāna* (see Question 52).

The individual *rājasik* aspects of the five *tan-mātras* produce the *karma-indriyas*, or sense organs of action: tongue (from space), hands (from air), legs (from fire), genitals (from water), and anus (from earth).

- The individual *tāmasik* aspects of the five *tan-mātras* undergo *pañchī-karaṇa* to form the five elements that make up the gross world.

  After *pañchī-karaṇa*, the total *tāmasik* aspects of the five *tan-mātras* combine to form the gross (physical) body.

50. What is *pañchī-karaṇa*, or the grossification process of the five elements?

According to *Advaita Vedānta*, *Brahman* alone is real and all else is unreal. The concept of creation is described as follows: From the one Source, *Brahman*, come forth the five elements and their combinations to create the phenomenal world. The process by which the five subtle elements (*pañcha-tan-mātras*) become the five gross elements (*pañcha-mahābhūtas*), which make up the gross world, is called the five-step division/combination process, or *pañchī-karaṇa*.

For further study, see *Tattva Bodha* by Ādi Shaṅkara, with commentary by Swami Tejomayananda.

51. What is a human being's external and internal composition?

As scientists analyze the objective world without, so too, the philosophers and seekers of Truth study the subjective world within. The *rishis* (seers) discovered that the human being is composed of:

Three bodies:

- *Sthūla-sharīra*: gross physical body

- *Sūkshma-sharīra*: subtle body (mind and intellect)
- *Kāraṇa-sharīra*: causal body

Four composite personalities:

- Physical
- Mental
- Intellectual
- Spiritual

Five sheaths, or layers (corresponding with the three bodies):

- *Annamaya-kosha*, or food sheath: the physical body that is born of food, is sustained by food, and returns to the elements to become food again
- *Prāṇamaya-kosha*, or vital-air sheath: made up of the five *prāṇa*s, or physiological activities (see Question 52)
- *Manomaya-kosha*, or mental sheath: the mind, which is the seat of emotions
- *Vijñānamaya-kosha*, or intellectual sheath: the intellect, which is the seat of discrimination and judgment
- *Ānandamaya-kosha*, or bliss sheath: the state of dreamless deep sleep, which is the seat of blissful ignorance

52. Describe in detail the three bodies that make up a human being.

The gross body, or *sthūla-sharīra*, is:

- Composed of the five elements, or *pañcha-mahābhūta*s (space, air, fire, water, earth), which have undergone the *pañchī-karaṇa* process (see Question 50)
- Determined by the results of past actions
- The tenement in which to experience joy (*sukha*), sorrow (*duḥkha*), etc.
- Subject to the six modifications: existence (as a fetus), birth, growth, change, decay, and death
- The basis of relationships like son, father, mother, daughter, etc.

The subtle body, or *sūkshma-sharīra*, is:

- Composed of the five elements, or *pañcha-mahābhūta*s (space, air, fire, water, earth), which have not undergone the *pañchī-karaṇa* process
- Born as and determined by the results of past actions
- The instrument for experiencing pleasure, pain, etc.
- Comprised of 17 aspects:
    - 5 *jñāna-indriya*s, or sense organs of perception: ears, skin, eyes, tongue, nose (the respective functional aspects or powers of hearing, touching, seeing, tasting, and smelling)
    - 5 *karma-indriya*s, or sense organs of action: tongue, hands, legs, genitals, anus (the respective functional aspects or powers of speech, grasping, locomotion, reproduction, and excretion)

- 5 *prāṇas*: *prāṇa* (inhalation), *apāna* (exhalation), *vyāna* (circulation), *udāna* (the capacity to entertain new thoughts and leave the body at the time of death), *samāna* (assimilation); it should be noted that *prāṇa* and *apāna* are not restricted to respiratory activities alone

- 2 inner instruments: the mind and intellect (two functions of the same equipment; see Question 53)

The causal body, or *kāraṇa-sharīra*, is:

- Inexplicable, beginningless, and in the form of *avidyā* (ignorance of Reality)

- The abode of all *vāsanā*s (tendencies that compel the *jīva* to take another birth) and thus the cause for the gross and subtle bodies

- Unqualified in form and free from thought modifications

53. What is the *antaḥ-karaṇa*, or inner equipment?

The *antaḥ-karaṇa* is the inner equipment of cognition. Its "mind-stuff" or "thought-stuff" has four facets:

- *Manas*: mind (expresses as indecisiveness and agitation)

- *Buddhi*: intellect (expresses as decisiveness and rational thinking)

- *Chitta*: memory

- *Ahaṁkāra*: I-thought (sense of individuality, or ego)

54. What is the mind and what are its different aspects?

Mind is the flow of thoughts, or *vritti*s. The basis of all thoughts is the I-thought, or *aham vritti*. All thoughts other than the I-thought are known as *idam vritti*. The mind stays in five states:

- *Kshipta*: restless and distracted, wandering from one object to another

- *Mūḍha*: deluded, absorbed in pleasure, or blinded by passion

- *Vikshipta*: restless and distracted by one object

- *Ekāgra*: single-pointed

- *Niruddha*: controlled, with cessation of all thoughts, as in deep sleep

55. What are the waking, dream, and deep sleep states, and what is the state beyond time and space?

Our three states of experience are known as the *avasthā-traya*:

- The waking state (*jāgrat*)

- The dream state (*svapna*)

- The deep sleep state (*sushupti*)

Transcending these three is the state of God-consciousness called *Turīya*, one's real nature of inherent divinity. This fourth state is the permanent state of bliss, whereas the former three are temporary states of modification.

Jāgrat-avasthā, or waking state: When the *jīva*, or individual self, through his 14 instruments (five sense organs of action, five sense organs of perception, and four facets of the *antaḥ-karaṇa*) perceives the gross objects in their respective fields and interacts with them, the *jīva* is in the waking state.

Svapna-avasthā, or dream state: The world of experience projected by the mind, as a result of impressions gathered consciously or unconsciously in the waking state, is *svapna*, or the dream state.

Sushupti-avasthā, or deep sleep state: This is the state of blissful ignorance. When all instruments cease activity and there is total absence of differentiated knowledge, when even the mind does not function, when Consciousness remains without the duality of subject and object, then the *jīva* is said to be in the *sushupti*, or deep sleep state.

Example using the BMI Chart (see Question 56): The BMI and PFT are totally withdrawn from all OET, but since *avidyā* (ignorance, in the form of *vāsanās*) has not been lifted, there is no awareness of pure Consciousness (Om).

Turīya: *Turīya* is the state of pure Consciousness, where the body, mind, intellect, sense of individuality, objects, emotions, and thoughts do not exist; where *avidyā* is transcended; and where one's true nature as *Brahman* reveals.

56. What is the BMI Chart?

ॐ

V

↓

B M I

↓ ↓ ↓

P F T

↓ ↓ ↓

O E T

Swami Chinmayananda developed the BMI Chart to simplify the concepts of *Advaita Vedānta* and describe the relationships among the absolute Reality, the individual self, and the relative world.

The absolute Reality (ॐ, or Om) expresses as the individual self (*jīva*, or PFT) because of the force of accumulated *vāsanā*s (V). The Self (Om), through the instruments of body, mind, and intellect (BMI), as if takes on the roles of perceiver, feeler, and thinker (PFT), and interacts with the world of objects, emotions, and thoughts (OET). When the individual transcends all *vāsanā*s, he realizes his true Self. For further study, see *Self-Unfoldment* by Swami Chinmayananda.

57. Who is the *jīva*, who is *Īshvara*, and what is the relationship between the two?

Jīva is defined as *avidyā-upādhiḥ san ātmā jīva iti uchyate*, "The *Ātman*, as if conditioned by the limitation known as ignorance, is called *jīva*." It is this individual *jīva* that goes in search of happiness with its *vāsanā*s from life to life, body to body.

Īshvara is defined as *māyā-upādhiḥ san īshvara iti uchyate*, "Awareness, as if conditioned by *māyā*, is called *Īshvara*." *Īshvara* is another term for God, used with reference to the creation, maintenance, and destruction of the universe.

- *Jīva*: limited in knowledge, power, and pervasiveness; bound and controlled by *māyā*

- *Īshvara*: infinite and unlimited in knowledge, power, and pervasiveness; wielder and controller of *māyā*

It is important to note that both, *jīva* and *Īshvara*, are, in essence, *Brahman* alone. They are described differently only with respect to their associated conditionings.

58. What is *māyā*?

Sarva Upanishad describes *māyā* as that power which is beginningless and contains within it the seeds to create the entire universe. It is neither real (because it has no power or independent existence separate from *Brahman*), nor unreal (because it is apparently perceived and experienced in this world through its expressions of *āvaraṇa* [veiling, nonapprehension] and *vikshepa* [agitation, misapprehension]). For further study, see *Tattva Bodha*.

59. If the *jīva* is bound by *māyā*, yet is responsible for the choices that determine his destiny, how much of his life is fate and how much of it is free will?

Both fate (destiny) and free will are equally at play in our lives at any given time, in past, present, or future. The cycle can be described as follows: Our past actions (free will) determine what we face in the present; this is our self-made destiny. How we face our situations in the present is our free will and this again determines the fate of our future. Basically, we create a blueprint of our future based on our actions in the present.

It is important to note that we ourselves qualify and limit our free will by the *vāsanā*s we cultivate through our actions and habits. There is no point in trying to determine the ratio of free will and destiny at play in any situation. What is needed is to break the cycle by exhausting or transcending all current *vāsanā*s without creating any new ones.

60. If the *jīva* is the maker of his own destiny, is there any value in praying to *Īshvara*?

Yes. Prayers full of intense devotion and faith do work, for they invoke the divine power present in each of us. Prayers are not answered based on God's whims and fancies or biases and prejudices. Devotees invoke *Īshvara*'s grace or power through their sincerity, self-effort, faith, and devotion.

61. What is *Brahman*?

Brahman is the One changeless Truth or Reality. *Brahman* literally means "That which is bigger than the biggest" (and is subtler than the subtlest). *Brahman* cannot be defined, described, or conceived by the intellect. However, to convey at least some idea at the intellectual level, the Upanishads give pointers such as:

- *Satyam* (Truth): that which does not change in the three periods of time (past, present, and future); despite the appearance of the world of names and forms, conditioned by time, space, and causation, *Brahman* remains changeless; changeless Existence is *Sat* or *Satyam*

- *Jñānam* (Knowledge): self-effulgent Consciousness or Awareness (*Chit*); the principle of knowing without a knower or known

- *Anantam* (Infinite): that which does not have a beginning or an end

- *Ānanda* (Bliss): conscious happiness; the state of unconditioned, objectless (independent) joy, where happiness is not dependent on anything or anyone in the world

The word *Brahman* is the *Tat* aspect when meditating on the *mahāvākya* "*Tat tvam asi*," or "That thou art" (see Question 27).

62. What additional terms, other than *Ātman* and *Brahman*, are used to indicate a human being's true nature?

- *Sākshī*: *Sākshī*, or Witness, refers to the pure Awareness that witnesses the world but does not get affected or involved.

  Example: The sun illumines the universe but remains unaffected by it and does not consider whether it is illumining a palace, a hospital, a prison, or a temple.

Sākshī is beyond time, space, and the triad of experiencer, experiencing, and experienced. It witnesses all thoughts, words, and deeds without interfering with them or being affected by them. This is because there is nothing in the universe other than It.

- *Kūṭastha*: *Kūṭa* literally means "anvil." All objects that come in contact with the anvil change their form, but the anvil itself remains unchanged; so too, *Ātman* remains the changeless substratum upon which changes play. The realization that pure Consciousness alone is, is the state of *Kūṭastha.*

- *Pratyagātman*: When the Self shines free from all limiting adjuncts as a brilliant, homogenous mass of Consciousness, as Existence-Knowledge-Bliss (*Sat-Chit-Ānanda*), it is called *Pratyagātman. Pratyagātman* literally means "inner Self" and indicates the *jīva*'s true nature of Consciousness.

The word *Pratyagātman* is the *tvam* aspect when meditating on the *mahāvākya "Tat tvam asi,"* or "That thou art" (see Question 27).

63. What is spiritual liberation?

Moksha, or liberation, is freedom from all bondage through knowledge of the Self. Bondage refers to the sense of, and identification with, the limitations of body, mind, intellect, and time, space, object. We are ever free, but are only deluded that we are bound in the cycle of birth and death. Self-realization, or *moksha*, can be attained while living in the world (*jīvan-mukti*), upon departure from the gross body (*videha-mukti*), or in stages after leaving the gross body (*krama-mukti*). For further study, see Adi Shankaracharya's *Vivekachūḍāmaṇi.*

64. What causes an individual to consider himself bound?

Avidyā (ignorance) is the cause. Ignorance of one's true nature results in the false sense of separateness, incompleteness, and limitation. *Avidyā* expresses itself as the three *guṇa*s and results in identification with the body, mind, and intellect, which leads the individual to believe that he is limited and bound by time, space, and object.

Example: Due to ignorance, I identify myself with the misconceptions that I am limited in knowledge, that I am born and therefore will die, and that I need other things or beings to be happy. Such identification and sense of individuality is bondage. Nonrecognition of my true nature (nonapprehension) leads to the superimposition or imagination of who I am (misapprehension).

65. How can the knowledge of the Self be imparted if the Self is not an object?

The guru, in keeping with the *shāstra*s (scriptures), adopts a peculiar methodology of teaching, wherein he uses the two-fold process of *anvaya-vyatireka* (the principle of variable-invariable or inclusion-exclusion) and *adhyāropa-apavāda* (the principle of deliberate superimposition-negation) to indicate to the disciple his true nature, the Truth behind the Upanishadic declaration, *Tat tvam asi*, "That thou art."

- *Anvaya*, or the variable factor, revealing the nature of *tvam*, "you": The identification of Consciousness with the body, mind, and intellect provides us with experiences strong enough for us to conclude that the "I" in us is the body, mind, and intellect. When we say, "I am thin," or "I am agitated," or "I am intelligent," the respective variable factors are the body, mind, and intellect, by which we feel we have been conditioned.

- *Vyatireka*, or the invariable factor, revealing the nature of *Tat*, "That": The invariable factor is the very core of our being, pure Consciousness, which is aware of all the variable factors, but is unaffected by them. When seen from the standpoint of creation, the variable factors of birth, sustenance, and death take place in the presence of the one invariable Source behind the cycle of creation.

Thus, the goal is to differentiate between the variable and invariable, and disidentify with the variable so that the invariable alone is revealed as one's true Self.

- *Adhyāropa*, or deliberate superimposition: The guru and the scriptures initially give a seeming reality to the ignorant notions that we entertain, without negating them, such as our notions of "I" and the relative world.

- *Apavāda*, or the subsequent negation: Once ignorance is recognized as the cause of the I-notion and the world, and these notions are negated, the Self reveals.

Example: As children, we are taught that the sky is blue (*adhyāropa*). Later, we are taught that the sky does not actually have any color (*apavāda*). So too, we initially study in depth about *jīva-jagat-Īshvara*, the law of karma, etc. (*adhyāropa*). Later, we learn that all differentiation and sense of separateness is to be negated (*apavāda*) because *Brahman* (Oneness) alone is.

66. What is the difference between self-hypnotism and Self-realization?

All hypnotic effects are temporary; realization of the eternal Self is not. The process of meditation can be considered as dehypnotizing ourselves from our attachments and identifications. This process leads to the final rediscovery of the unconditioned Self.

67. What are the three direct means of knowledge for Self-realization?

According to Vedanta, the three direct means of knowledge that help the seeker attain Self-realization are:

- *Shravaṇa*: listening to spiritual teachings with faith and reverence

- *Manana*: based on our *shravaṇa*, logical reflection on, and clarification of, all doubts

- *Nididhyāsana*: contemplation in order to arrive at a firm conviction and live according to it

All other spiritual practices—chanting, worship, pilgrimages, service, etc.—help purify and channel the mind, and are the indirect means of knowledge for Self-realization.

68. What is meditation?

Meditation, in its subtlest import in Advaita Vedanta, refers to the state of pure Consciousness, where the duality of subject and object, the triad of experiencer, experiencing, and experienced, and the plurality of time, space, and object do not exist. Meditation is seen as the ultimate goal: Self-awareness.

Meditation is also commonly used today as a verb. It is often understood as a mere relaxation exercise; however, it has deeper significance for sincere spiritual seekers who practice meditation as the contemplative means to attain Self-realization. In the case of the seeker, meditation refers to the conscious process of quieting the mind to ultimately know, and abide in, the Self.

Other Sanskrit terms used for this process are *dhāraṇā*, *dhyāna*, *samādhi* (see Question 71). Swami Chinmayananda, in his text *Meditation & Life*, states: "When the mind's thoughts have been nourished by study, and rendered quiet and peaceful by *japa*, to rest the hushed mind at the altar of the Self in a thrilled mood of choiceless contemplation, is meditation (*dhyāna*)." For further study, see *Meditation & Life* and *Art of Contemplation* by Swami Chinmayananda, and *Meditation: A Vision* by Swami Tejomayananda.

69. How many kinds of votaries are there among those who seek God?

Lord Krishṇa names four types of votaries (people who turn to God) in *Gītā* 7.16:

- *Ārta*: a person in distress
- *Arthārthī*: a person seeking wealth and worldly possessions
- *Jijñāsu*: a person seeking higher knowledge
- *Jñānī*: a person of wisdom (who turns to God in pure love, not seeking anything)

70. Who is a *yogī*?

The word *yogī* comes from the root *yuj*, which means "to unite." He who has dissolved his lower self in the higher Self, that is, merged his individual consciousness with the universal Consciousness, is a *yogī*. The spiritual seeker becomes a *yogī* by first understanding the nature of the Self and then practicing various disciplines to realize the Self.

71. What are the prescribed paths to reach the stage of a *yogī*?

There are many prescribed paths, all leading to the same goal: the path of knowledge (*jñāna yoga*), the path of devotion (*bhakti yoga*), and the path of service or dedicated action (*karma yoga*). Additionally, the path of *rāja yoga* or *ashṭāṅga yoga* is exhaustively described in the yoga aphorisms of Sage Patanjali. The "eight limbs" of *ashṭāṅga yoga* are the eight steps to Self-realization:

- *Yama*: *ahiṁsā* (nonviolence in thought, word, and deed), *satya* (truthfulness), *āsteya* (not stealing), *brahmacharya* (celibacy or self-control), and *aparigraha* (not aggrandizing or hoarding)

- *Niyama*: *shaucha* (purity of body and mind), *santosha* (contentment), *tapa* (penance or sacrifice for a higher goal), *svādhyāya* (self-study), and *Īshvara-praṇidhāna* (surrender and dedication to God)

- *Āsana*: postures conducive to purifying and balancing energy channels in the body and mind

- *Prāṇāyāma*: control of the *prāṇik* forces (systematic breathing is only a part of these forces; see Question 52)

- *Pratyāhāra*: restraining the senses; withdrawing the senses from their respective objects

- *Dhāraṇā*: steadying the mind

- *Dhyāna*: contemplation

- *Samādhi*: direct experience of the state of infinite Bliss

For further study on yoga, see *The Holy Geeta* by Swami Chinmayananda. For further study on *samādhi*, including *savikalpa* and *nirvikalpa samādhi*, see Swami Chinmayananda's commentary on *Vivekachūḍāmaṇi* by Ādi Shaṅkara.

72. Who is a guru?

Gu represents darkness, or ignorance of the highest Reality, and *ru* represents removal of that ignorance. Thus, the guru is one who removes the disciple's ignorance and allows the Truth to be revealed.

In *Vivekachūḍāmaṇi*, Ādi Shaṅkara describes the guru as "he who is well-versed in the scriptures, sinless, unafflicted by desires, a full knower of the Supreme, calm as the fire that has burned up its fuel, a boundless ocean of mercy that needs no cause to express, and an intimate friend to those who have surrendered unto him."

Vedanta teaches that the guru, who is one with God, or *Brahman*, is not just a physical entity. He is the ever-present, inner guiding force within every seeker. Thus, the guru's physical or subtle form manifests as needed solely for the benefit of the disciple.

73. Who is a disciple?

A disciple (*shishya*) is one who subjects himself to the guru's discipline. A disciple is one who is devoted to the guru, implicitly follows the guru's teachings, and serves the guru for the sole purpose of enlightenment. The guru guides the disciple as needed to progress on his spiritual journey to go beyond *saṁsāra* (the cycle of birth and death) and attain Self-realization.

The spiritual relationship between guru and *shishya* is similar to that of a parent and child. Parents give the child life, but the guru gives the disciple freedom from life and death by guiding him to realize his own true nature. Thus, the disciple can never repay the guru for this debt.

74. What are the qualifications of a spiritual seeker?

Sādhana-chatushṭaya is the set of four qualifications to be developed by a sincere seeker in order to study Vedanta and realize the Self. The four qualifications are: *viveka*, *vairāgya*, *shamādi-shaṭ-sampatti*, and *mumukshutva*.

- *Viveka*: *nitya-anitya-vastu vivekaḥ*, "discrimination between the Eternal and the ephemeral;" a firm conviction of the mind that *Brahman* alone is real (unchanging) and the universe of names and forms is unreal (changing)

- *Vairāgya*: *iha-amutra-phala-bhoga-virāgaḥ*, "nonattachment to the fruits of one's actions in this life or the next;" leads one to renounce cravings for transitory enjoyments

- *Shamādi-shaṭ-sampatti*: "the six-fold wealth [attributes to be cultivated], beginning with *shama*, etc.":

  - *Shama*: control over the mind; detaching the mind from sense objects (not allowing sense objects to enter the mind)
  - *Dama*: control over the sense organs; withdrawing the senses from sense objects (not allowing the sense organs to go out to the sense objects)

  - *Uparati*, or *uparama*: inner withdrawal, where the mind is no longer affected by the external world of objects

  - *Titikshā*: forbearance; patiently persevering in the face of all afflictions and difficulties, without grievance or worry

  - *Shraddhā*: faith; firm conviction in the guru, Lord, scriptures, and Self

  - *Samādhāna*: single-pointedness in scriptural studies, reflection, and contemplation

- *Mumukshutva*: "intense yearning for liberation" from all bondage; longing for freedom from identification with the three instruments (body, mind, and intellect), the three states (waking, dream, and deep sleep), and the three limitations (time, space, and object)

Ādi Shaṅkara says in *Vivekachūḍāmaṇi*, "He who has a keen memory, enough knowledge of the world outside, an understanding of the world within, who believes in and stands up for the scriptures and can refute arguments against them—such a one is fit for receiving *Ātma-vidyā* (Self-knowledge, *Brahma-vidyā*)."

An *adhikārī* is thus a qualified student who is fit to receive *Brahma-vidyā* from the guru. Such a person:

- Has general knowledge of the Vedas and similar scriptures

- Has a pure mind
- Is endowed with *sādhana-chatushṭaya*
- Performs *nitya karma*s (daily duties) and *naimittika karma*s (special duties)
- Avoids *kāmya karma*s (desire-born actions) and *nishiddha karma*s (wrongful actions)
- Observes *prāyaschitta karma*s (acts of penance to correct or improve oneself) when necessary

PART FIVE

WHY RELIGION?

PART FIVE: WHY RELIGION?

75. Why does religion seem to appeal only to the minority?

As long as the majority of humankind searches for happiness and freedom on the physical plane, religion will appeal only to the minority. With the development of his mental and intellectual faculties, the aspirant's spirit of inquiry grows. Religion provides an inquiring mind with the highest goal of life and the paths to reach it. For those who are on the sensual level and have not yet outgrown their baser tendencies, religion will not have an immediate appeal.

76. What is meant by the statement, "Hinduism is tolerant"?

Dr. S. Radhakrishnan (former President of India) said, "Hinduism is wholly free from the strange obsession . . . that the acceptance of a particular religious metaphysic is necessary for salvation and nonacceptance thereof is a heinous sin meriting eternal punishment in hell. Hindus do not proselytize. They do not lay exclusive claims to salvation, and they do not believe that God will be pleased by the wholesale slaughter of those of His creatures whose beliefs are mistaken."

77. What is the relationship between science and religion?

Science and religion are interrelated, so when either disowns the other, there is decay in society. In order to establish harmony, society should embrace both science and religion.

Objective science presents a view of life through the study of the constantly changing world. But the human being cannot achieve complete happiness through scientific advancements alone. Subjective science, or spirituality, presents a way of life through the introspective study of the unchanging Reality and the means to attain that Reality. Spirituality, Vedanta in particular, teaches fundamental values and their practical applications in order to achieve the goal of complete and permanent happiness.

Science raises the standard of living, whereas religion raises the standard of life. Science and religion can vitalize each other, for material advancement through scientific methods will be fruitless without the nobler values of healthy living that religion teaches. Just as mere knowledge of architecture and a perfect blueprint cannot, without quality materials, create a strong structure, so too, a materially advanced society that does not adhere to value-based living cannot truly progress. Man can attain great heights by recognizing the real worth and utility of both science and religion.

78. How do we discover why God created this world?

One can look at this question in different ways:

- Even in scientific investigations, the "why" remains unanswered (why the sun, why gravity, and so on). When it comes to Nature's laws, motive-hunting is beyond the realm of science. This question should be asked of God, for He alone can answer it fully.

- On the path of *sādhanā*, when the mind's impurities have been removed and *māyā* has been transcended, the Truth will be revealed and all questions and doubts will be cleared.

- To attain the state of Oneness, the entire triad of the questioner (ego), questioning, and questioned must dissolve. In Oneness, who questions whom?

- Because the world is constantly changing, it cannot be defined as "real." How can we ask why the world was created when the created world is but an illusion? When the equipments of experience are transcended, the projected world merges into the One and there is no world to be questioned.

79. How does Vedanta help a person achieve happiness?

An individual's life is a continuity of experiences, driven by a constant yearning to achieve complete and lasting happiness, a fuller and deeper peace. To live harmoniously, one must have right understanding of oneself and the world.

Vedanta does not teach indifference to sorrow, poverty, injustice, etc., but does teach how wrong estimation of the world and superimposition of false values on things, beings, and situations can result in unhappy and painful experiences. Vedanta teaches one how to readjust one's view of, and relationship with, the world, in order to ultimately realize the Self.

PART SIX

QUESTIONS AND ANSWERS WITH SWAMI CHINMAYANANDA

PART SIX: QUESTIONS AND ANSWERS WITH SWAMI CHINMAYANANDA

Excerpts from a questionnaire by Bharatiya Vidya Bhavan (circa *1975)*

80. Is the influence of religion on the masses declining? If not, how can we account for corruption and other such pointers that indicate widespread deterioration in ethical and moral values?

All those who have eyes can vividly see that religion in India is today more popular than ever before. Famous temples are overflowing with pilgrims; new temples are mushrooming all over; temple construction committees are spontaneously rising up even in the most distant corners of shy villages, and they are sincerely struggling to find funds and materials for rebuilding and renovating the neglected and dilapidated old shrines.

Daily newspapers all over the country are announcing in their columns dozens of spiritual talks and religious functions. Religion is rampant as never before. This is, to an extent, true all over the world. The widespread sense of insecurity, political and economic, compels the human being to run to religion, to use it perhaps as a crutch.

Honestly, I do not believe that most of the immorality and corruption found in the world is caused by any lack of religion. Immorality and corruption are, at best, the by-products of unintelligent laws, general scarcity, rise in population, and the consequent unnatural, crowded living conditions in impossibly large metropolitan centers. And certainly in India, the sudden change in our values, brought about by the spirit of secularism, is also nibbling away at the confused hearts of the illiterate and uneducated. If we can lace this freshly streaming spirit of religion in our country with at least a dash of deeper philosophical and cultural depth, a bigger change in the moral flavor of our social life will surely follow.

81. The traditional charge against Hinduism is that it is fatalistic and that it inhibits progress by making people slaves to the belief in the inevitability of whatever is to happen. How far is this true? What is the basis of such an accusation, which is being advanced even today by well-meaning and highly educated people?

The idea of destiny is very much a part of Hinduism, and as a truth, it cannot be denied. The subtle thinkers, our *rishi*s, while analyzing and studying life in the raw, in the light of their own subjective experiences of the spiritual Essence, came to the honest conclusion that there is an inevitable continuity in all happenings. The present is naturally a product of the entire past. Therefore, the past orders, controls, and governs the present. "This is destiny!" cry all hasty students.

This hasty conclusion is what the Western missionaries have gathered from their hurry-burry studies of our deep and profound thought. They translated and criticized. And these criticisms are available in well-bound, attractive volumes at many universities and public libraries. The modern, educated Indian reads these books. The thoughtful reader gets shocked by the conflicts therein, but the thoughtless reader comes to blindly believe all that he gathers from these incompetent, second-hand, smothered ideas. The hasty Western student understands only one-half of our law of karma, and those who misunderstand it preach the hopeless philosophy of "destiny" as being the essence of Hindu thought.

"The present is the product of the past" is not all that the law of karma declares. Half a thought in any philosophy can become a dangerous, false statement. The law of karma, when completely declared, insists upon a scientifically unassailable truth: "The present is the product of the past, and the future is the past modified in the present." The present with reference to the past is already "destiny," but by the very texture of our present thoughts and by the quality of our present actions—self-effort—we are ordering and building our future. This larger implication is an organic part of the law of karma and cannot ever be separated without destroying the truth of the entire concept. In short, what we meet in life is "destiny" (*prārabdha*) and how we meet what we meet in life is self-effort (*purushārtha*).

The present criticism that "it [destiny] inhibits progress by making people slaves to the belief in the inevitability of whatever is to happen" cannot stand in the light of any deep inquiry. The present is ordered by the past; therefore, the present is inevitable. In the forenoon, I consume a lot of salt; in the afternoon, it is inevitable that I will feel thirsty. It is sheer wisdom to recognize the present as the effect of some cause or causes initiated in the past. Wisdom is the antidote for all confusion and the solace for all fear.

Historically the Hindus would not have survived as a cultural unit after all these centuries of persecution and political slavery but for this deep understanding and their consequent unshakeable heroism and inner composure in the face of all their trials. Maybe we must now re-educate the public in the positive aspect of the law of karma: that thought by thought and action by action, we are sculpting our future.

82. It is said that the greatest strength of Hinduism is its breadth of outlook and that this is also its greatest weakness, in that there are very few common prescribed religious observances obligatory for all, as in other religions. Is it necessary and possible to outline certain basic, minimum observances for all Hindus?

This is a very delicate and sensitive area, and no one should dash into it with any hasty remedy. Hinduism is geared toward producing saints, evolving sages, and raising masters. Spiritual perfection in the individual is the goal. Beautifying the mind, uplifting the vision to the highest, and thereby coming to manifest the glory of the flame of Existence, so as to enrich and enthrall the world around him—this is an art. And indeed, art can grow only in freedom.

Religions, at their lower levels, aim at organizing society and harnessing the emotional fervor of the population, thus generating a kind of social militancy, which is, no doubt, good for the political and economic well-being of a community. However, the sorrows that such a society can spawn are indeed calamitous. The pages of human history may have been cleaner if not for such religions and their deadly fanaticisms. Whether it is the Christian War of the Roses and other bloody battles waged, or the Islamic *jihad*s, or the Shaivite and Vaishnavite conflicts in the South, or the feuds between the *Ārya Samājī*s and the *Sanātanī*s in the North—every one of them is an example of the confrontations that inevitably arise when religions are organized and religious thought is walled in by dogma and rituals.

I am not against organization. I am very much conscious that I myself am the head of an organization with a vision, [and this organization] is growing every day as a result of my personal, tireless endeavors. Organization is unavoidably needed. We need churches, mosques, temples, and other such institutions. Large masses of people congregating therein can thereby develop in their actions and thoughts a rhythm at once loving and divine. But in prescribing these strict religious schemes of service, we must grow truly sensitive to feel how far we should go and not become insistent. Otherwise, we will destroy the spontaneity in the seeker, which many other religions do. Those who no longer need the warm protection of a religious institution must be able to walk out of its motherly embrace and seek their own independent and fuller expressions in the quest divine.

I believe the present system is more than sufficient for this purpose. All that we need is a team of intelligent, educated interpreters who can update the truths of our philosophy and religious texts to fit the thought patterns of our own times. If the long-term plan is to train such a cadre of priests, then, as a short-term policy, I would strongly recommend that such literature, in the form of pamphlets, be distributed to the masses through the temples, as a part of the usual *prasāda*, especially on sacred days and festive occasions.

83. Will the fundamental values of Hinduism be in any way affected by the eradication of casteism, toward which a concerted effort is being made now, on all levels? If Harijans, who constitute a sizable population among Hindus, are made to feel that their religion exposes them to ridicule, how are they to love that religion? In other words, how can all sections of Hindus be made to take equal interest in, and have the same sense of belonging to, their religion?

"Caste-ism" has no place in Hinduism. The word "caste" indicates a scientific classification of man's inner personality, which is universal and true for all times. Every one of us expresses in one of three distinct moods (*sattva, rajas, tamas*) due to the preponderance of one over the other two. Based on these moods, the human mind functions in four different grades (*varṇa*s). These psychological classifications are called castes. In fact, caste only shows how you are cast.

When a thought, however good it may be, is with an individual for a long period of time, his vested interests come to abuse it, and the distorted thought, in time, often grows to become an ugly veil in society. Casteism is not permitted, while castes are inevitable. There are *brāhmaṇa*s (Brahmins) in America as much as *shūdra*s in Rome. Where in the world can you not find honest, ethical, clean thinkers (*brāhmaṇa*s); enthusiastic and tireless leaders of men in the political field (*kshatriya*s); commercial men (*vaishya*s); and labor-oriented persons (*shūdra*s)? But not to recognize that they are all different aspects of the one infinite Lord is a pernicious conspiracy brought into society by the covetous. Such things happen around the world when leaders try to guard their own selfish interests. The sad and unjust condition of the African-Americans in America is a case in point. Theirs is but a history of 200 years. The evil that we [in India] are faced with has a history of about 3,000 years.

Yet, in our [India's] 30 years of independence, we have, in our Constitution, updated the rights and privileges of the Harijans to be at par with the Brahmins. True, the emotional integration is not yet complete, especially in the interior conservative villages. But the progress that we have already made is phenomenal. We shall continue the same policy, and perhaps we must intelligently modulate it to bring about some more self-respect and self-sufficiency in the younger generation, which has already been redeemed. They [the younger generation] should not lean too much on the government or play an endless tune of complaints. It is time that they show their political responsibility and social maturity. Now they are flooding into schools and colleges. If we can end, through our education system, our political attitude of strict untouchability and unapproachability toward our cultural traditions and religious literature, we could perhaps re-educate our brothers much quicker. They have suffered in neglect not because there was any scriptural sanction for it, but because of an error in reading and interpreting the pregnant [scriptural] statements, or perhaps even because of a deliberate act of political maneuvering by those who were then in power, wanting to protect and perpetuate their vested interests.

84. Hinduism has always renewed or revitalized itself according to the needs of the times. In today's context, are any corrective measures called for? If so, who will bring them about, and how can they be brought about and made acceptable to the masses?

When a culture is alive, it will create its own answers to all the insistent demands of the historical period and the evils of that period. Our culture has done it many a time in the past. Vyāsa, Buddha, Shaṅkara, Rāmānuja, Madhvāchārya, Vivekananda, Narayana Guru, are a few examples. In the same way, the new age will create its own masters.

When we look around, we see that this rejuvenation is being accomplished all over again. The stupendous activities of pioneers like Swami Sivananda, Aurobindo, Ramana Maharshi, Swami Ram Das of Kanjangad, Neem Karoli Baba, and others; the gigantic efforts of *Shrī* Satya Sai Baba; the benign services of institutions like Bharatiya Vidya Bhavan, Gita Press of Gorakhpur, and others; [all these,] like the organized, disciplined, and intelligently maneuvered programs of

Chinmaya Mission, now spread all over the country and abroad. These are answers to the throb that is now being felt within our Hindu community. To say that Hinduism has not shown any response to the needs of our times is to be utterly blind to what is happening today not only in our country, but all around the world.

The emphasis is slowly shifting from ritualism to yoga and a deeper study of philosophy, [to prepare one] to enter into and explore the secrets of inner life through contemplation and meditation. To run schools and colleges in a general atmosphere of culture and religion, to give our growing generation a fair chance to judge for itself its own traditions and culture, to provide educated preachers who can preach religious and spiritual ideas with reference to our immediate social and economic needs, to spare some time on the air and space in the newspapers and journals to discuss constructively the practical ideas of *Bhagavad Gītā*, to revive through attractive programs people's enthusiasm to reach our temples for mass silent prayers—these are some of the programs I would strongly recommend, since these are the very programs I have been working on, indeed, very successfully, for many years.

85. Are fasting and such other dietary regulations necessary for leading a spiritual life? Is a guru essential for one to enter the spiritual path and attain the goal?

To withdraw the mind's wandering attention from the outer world of names and forms, and to redirect its attention steadily to the spring of all activities in one's own within, is spiritual seeking. To center our attention on this inner silence and tranquility, and to confront the world of happenings around, is spiritual life. Naturally, therefore, fasting becomes important, not necessarily as the non-eating of food, which we take in by the mouth, but as a strict discipline maintained in all our intakes—seeing, hearing, smelling, touching, even feeling and thinking.

The very fact that you are asking these questions clearly shows that we need teachers to teach us. Think for a moment: Is there anything that we do well today, with confidence or any amount of mastery, which has not been taught to us? If, for every perfect act in the world, in any department of activity, by anyone, we need the guidance of an instructor, then you can very well understand the need for a guru on the spiritual path, where we have to deal with the subtlest forces and the enormous confusions of the vehicle called the mind, and its moods called delusions.

86. Will mantras lose their sanctity if they are not chanted in Sanskrit? There are various *saṁskāra*s prescribed in Hinduism from birth to death. Many of these *saṁskāra*s are not being observed today. Should they not be revived?

Mantras are not mere words. That which uplifts us when we reflect on it is a mantra. So the sound symbol, or mantra, serves as the rails for the train of thought to smoke through and reach its destination of vivid and direct experience. Whatever be the language in which mantras are chanted, each individual will reflect upon them in his own native language. Thus, when an American chants *Shivoham*, he cannot reflect upon the significance of this mantra except in his own native tongue: "I am auspiciousness; I am Shiva." Therefore, what harm can there be in his mantra being in any language?

No doubt, Sanskrit is such a perfect language that the very vibrations of the words in the mantra have a soothing effect on the mind. Yet, this is but a very superficial gain as compared to the deep significance, divine glory, endless richness, fabulous beauty—the holiness and preciousness—of the meaning arrived at through reflection. Will anyone ever purchase a costly pearl necklace in order to have only its velvet container?

For the masses, celebrations and demonstrations have an impressive impact. Even a peace-loving country like ours must have military parades on Republic Day in order to reinforce the confidence of the masses in the might of the country. These *saṁskāra*s (rituals) have an effect, just as convocation assemblies, marriage ceremonies, the laying of foundation stones, the unveiling of statues, and the inaugurations of dams, etc. do. *Saṁskāras*, if conducted by all, should bring about a sense of discipline and a pride of belonging, providing a healthy reminder of the significant cultural meanings of these rituals to all those who attend such functions.

87. What is the role of rituals in religion? Are they to be discouraged?

Rituals are objective dramatizations of the subjective art of self-perfection; such ceremonious and attractive displays of rhythm and beauty cannot be eliminated from human life. Historically, it is true that whenever ritualism is removed, churches, mosques, and temples are closed down and replaced by military parades, nightclubs and their excesses, racecourse crowds, boxing galleries, etc. Let the public decide what they want. I would prefer that my countrymen have religious rituals entertaining them rather than the more dangerous and immoral alternatives.

88. What is your view regarding proselytization? If you were convinced that Hinduism has a great role to play in the world, would you consider proselytization?

Proselytizing is the cheap commercialism of religion. It is not sanctioned in Hinduism. We are enjoined only to propagate the spiritual science that is our inheritance. By gathering an understanding of the Hindu Upanishads and gaining a glimpse of the universal thoughts expounded by the *rishi*s therein, a Christian can perhaps become a better Christian, a Hindu surely a better Hindu. Such training gives the human mind a subtler vision to see clearly the eternal thoughts expounded by the spiritual masters and the silent content in their pregnant words.

Any individual must be welcomed into the fold of any faith to participate in its spiritual practices. But to convert a people as though they are manufactured goods to be stamped with trademarks and packed and stored away in churches, temples, or mosques is a repugnant idea, choking the very spirit of Hindu scientific thought. However, we have every right to receive our brothers back—Hindus who had, because of their own confusions or due to some cruel political and/or economic pressures, left us to embrace other faiths. This is not conversion. This is a return into the fold of those who lost their way and strayed for a time.

89. Are changes visible in Hinduism's doctrines and in the modes of individual and collective worship as a result of contact with the West?

Visible changes are recognizable in other faiths due to their contacts with Hinduism. Evidently, today Hinduism is shedding her light and imparting her fragrance to Western thought. And I must say that the reverse is not at all visible or true. The scientific thoughts of the West have recently confirmed our *japa* technique and the powers inherent in the *bīja-aksharas* (sacred syllables, mantras). This is the contribution of the transcendental meditation techniques of Mahesh Yogi; this elementary technique of *japa* in Hinduism has become the great transcendental meditation so popular in the West today.

The Christian authorities have started emphasizing more than ever the need for meditation. They are re-reading their Bible and discovering a sanction for yoga in the words of Jesus. It is not too infrequent nowadays to see church programs that include yoga practices. I am indicating these only to demonstrate the spectacular signs of Hindu influence now glaringly evident in the West. In short, Hinduism gave more in her casual trip to the West than what she herself accepted when she suffered the embrace of the West all these centuries.

And is it not true that Christianity in India has become more Hinduized? Is not Mother Mary now wearing a *sārī*? Don't we hear the sounds of cymbals from churches? Don't churches now smell more of incense? Don't we see oil lamps replacing candles? Are processions with Indian drums of Jesus on elephants not a common sight in India? Are not Christian priests now calling themselves swamis? Are not their monasteries now becoming ashrams? Have not even churches started being called temples? Is it not becoming fashionable now to have a Hindu name for every Thomas, John, Mary, and Anna?

I do not think Hinduism has anything to gain from the West. . . . We have much to give them. . . . They are taking. . . . And they must take more.

Hari Om

APPENDIX

Hindu scriptural literature is so vast and comprehensive that there is no branch of knowledge left uninvestigated by the great seers of India. The Hindu was never satisfied unless every question that he faced, be it material, scientific, religious, philosophical, or spiritual, was thoroughly discussed in all aspects to its irrefutable conclusion.

The lists and tables that follow will give insight into the progress of Indian thought through the ages, and will show how our forefathers relentlessly investigated the various fields of knowledge; discovered scientific, philosophic, and spiritual truths; enunciated and codified them in systematic treatises on various subjects; and bequeathed them to posterity. To them, Sanātana Dharma *meant the eternal values of life that they adhered to in all circumstances. For them, Hinduism was not a closed book, because in their profound wisdom, they recognized the fact that there is no limit to knowledge. Search. You will find. The more you search, the more you will find.*

\- Swami Chinmayananda

VEDAS

1. ***Rig (Ṛk) Veda*:** 432,000 *Saṁhitās*; 28 *Brāhmaṇas*; 42 Upanishads; total of 707,000 stanzas

2. ***Yajur Veda*:** 250,000 *Saṁhitās*; 32 *Brāhmaṇas*; 60 Upanishads; total of 455,000 stanzas

3. ***Sāma Veda*:** 600,000 *Saṁhitās*; 21 *Brāhmaṇas*; 90 Upanishads; total of 950,000 stanzas

4. ***Atharva Veda*:** 300,000 *Saṁhitās*; 11 *Brāhmaṇas*; 52 Upanishads; total of 480,000 stanzas

UPA-VEDAS

1. ***Āyurveda*:** *Chakrānuvesha* by Sanaka; original works attributed to Dhanvantarī, extant works by Charaka, Sushruta, and Vegabhaṭṭa (also a bacteriologist); the science of longevity

2. ***Dhanurveda*:** *Praveshāshṭa-prakāsham* by Prachetas; original works attributed to Bhrigu and Vishvāmitra; the science of warfare

3. ***Gandharva Veda*:** *Svarānuvāda* by Nārada; the science of music

4. ***Sthāpatya Veda*:** *Siddhāntopanyastha* by Ashvini Kumāras; the science of architecture

DARSHANAS: SCHOOLS OF PHILOSOPHY

1. ***Nyāya***: Svayambhū's *Prabhāntarīksha*, Sage Gautama's *Nyāya Sūtras*, *Tarka-saṅgraha*, *Bhāsha-parichheḍa*, *Siddhānta-muktāvali*; *Kusumāñjali* by Udāyanāchārya is an important work on this subject

2. ***Vaisheshika***: Kratu's *Darshanānubhava*; subsequent work by Kannāda Rishi

3. ***Sānkhya***: Original work is Mārīcha's *Anubhava*; subsequent authoritative work by Sage Kapila

4. ***Yoga***: Original treatise by Chyamana called *Vrithyājitharṇava*; subsequent works by Sage Patanjali, with elaborate commentaries by Bhoja Deva, Vāchaspati Mishra, Vijñāna Bhikshu, and Nāgoji Bhaṭṭa

5. ***Mīmāṁsā***: Original work Arthaprakāsha of Rishi Aṅgiras; subsequent work by Sage Jaimini; also called *Pūrva Mīmāṁsā* or *Karma Mīmāṁsā*

6. ***Vedānta***: Also called *Uttara Mīmāṁsā*; original work is said to be Lord Brahmā's *Prahīksha-pradīpa*; subsequent work is *Brahma Sūtras* by Veda Vyāsa

SHABDA SHĀSTRAS

1. *Shikshā*: Phonetics

Maheshvara's *Shikshā* and *Nārada Bhāshya* are also called *prātisākhyas* and total 172,000 stanzas. This subject is also dealt with in a chapter in *Taittirīya Āraṇyaka* and a book called *Māṇḍukī* Shikshā.

2. *Kalpa*: Design and Construction of Religious Sites

Devi's *Vyavasthānubhava* is the original treatise of 248,000 stanzas. Subsequently, several works on this subject came out of each of the four Vedas. Examples include:

- From *Rig Veda*: *Ashvalāyana*, *Shaṅkhāyana*, *Shaunaka*
- From *Sāma Veda*: *Masaka*, *Lātyāyana*, *Drahyāyana*
- From *Yajur Veda*: *Āpastamba*, *Satyāshaḍha*, *Hiraṇyakeshi*, *Mānava*, *Bharadvāja*, *Vathūla*, *Vyākhanāsha*, *Maitra*, *Kathā*, *Varāha*, etc. (from *Krishṇa Yajur Veda*), *Kātyāyana* (from *Shukla Yajur Veda*)
- From *Atharva Veda*: *Kaushitaka*

3. *Vyākaraṇa*: Grammar

First came the *Maheshvara Sūtras* and *Nārada Bhāshya*, totaling 100,000 stanzas. Thereafter came the *Pāṇinī Sūtras* (*Ashṭādhyāyī*, the world-renowned grammatical work that remains unparalleled to date and is accepted as such by Western scholars also) and Patanjali's *Mahābhāshya*, both of which are important and authoritative treatises.

There were other notable grammarians before Pāṇinī, namely, Apishali, Kashyapa, Gārgya, Galava, Chakravarman, Bharadvāja, Shakaṭāyana,

Sakālya, Senaka, and Sphoṭāyana. Kātyāyana was an outstanding grammarian after Pāṇinī.

4. *Nirukta*: Vedic Etymology

Gaṇesha's *Nirukta* and Shesha's *Bhāshya* comprise 55,000 stanzas. Subsequent work was done by Yāskāchārya. A well-known work is *Amara Kosha*, also known as *Nāma-liṅga-anushāsanam*, written by the world's first lexicographer, Amarasiṁha, a great scholar who flourished in the court of King Vikramāditya and who was a contemporary of the great poet Kālidāsa.

5. *Chhandas*: Prosody (Meter)

Vishṇu's *Chhandorṇava* is comprised of 172,000 stanzas. The subsequent work of *Chhanda Shāstra* came from Piṅgala. Many other works came later, including *Nidāna Sūtra*, *Shruta-bodha*, *Vāṇībhūshaṇa*, *Vritta-darpaṇa*, *Vritta-ratnākara*, *Vritta-kaumudī*, *Chhandomanjarī*, and *Savritha-tilaka*. *Chhandomanjarī* by Gaṅgādāsa is an important work on this subject.

The number of meters possible in Sanskrit poetry is an astronomical figure. The word for meter in Sanskrit is *vritta*. There are three types of *vritta*s: *sāma vritta, vishama vritta*, and *ardha-sāma vritta*. The categorization depends on whether the composition of each line in a four-line stanza is the same or different. For example, in *sāma vritta*s, the maximum number of letters in a line is 26. With 1-26 hard-sound (*guru*) and soft-sound (*laghu*) letters in each line, the maximum number of meter-permutations under *sāma vritta* is 87,108,864.

6. *Jyotisha*: Astronomy and Astrology

Sūrya's *Brihadāṅka-pradīpa* has 100,000 stanzas. The subsequent important works are *Āryabhaṭṭīya* by Āryabhaṭṭa, and *Sūrya Siddhānta* by Bhāskarāchārya. There are also treatises on the subject by Varāha Mihira, Gārga, and Brahmagupta.

ARTS AND SCIENCES

1. ***Akshara Laksha*:** Attributed to Sage Vālmīki; deals with the branches of mathematics: arithmetic, algebra, geometry, trigonometry, physics, and applied mathematics; consists of 50 chapters; acknowledges the earlier discoveries of Hanumān, Jaimini, Brihaspati, Kashyapa; also deals with geography, air/wind, electricity, mineralogy, and more

2. ***Artha Shāstra*:** Short treatise attributed to Sage Vyāsa, wherein he deals with more than 80 ways of earning wealth through *dhārmik* means; extant work attributed to Kauṭilya

3. ***Chitra Karma*:** Believed to have been authored by Bhīma; deals with the science of fine arts; 12 chapters with more than 200 sketches; explains a novel method by which an artist can create the complete figure of a person after having seen only a portion of his body

4. ***Dhātu Vāda*:** Believed to have been written by Ashvini Kumāras; deals with the science of alchemy and the conversion of baser metals into gold; a treatise on *dhātu*s, or primary substances, and their reactions and combinations

5. ***Gaja Shāstra*:** Attributed to Kumārasvāmī; deals with the behavior and characteristics of elephants; gives methodology to categorize elephants on the basis of certain body marks

6. ***Kāla Nirṇaya*:** Attributed to Lord Kārtikeya; deals with the concept of time, auspicious and inauspicious occasions, limitations of time and its measurements, and the presiding deities of various dates, constellations, etc.

7. ***Lakshaṇa Shāstra*:** Attributed to Sage Shakaṭāyana; deals with the determination of gender in both animate and inanimate creation; Babhru Muni's work *Kanyā Lakshaṇa* lists characteristics of an

unwed girl that can be used to reveal her future, family life, children, prosperity, chastity, etc.

8. ***Shakuna Shāstra*:** Sage Gārga's detailed treatise on omens or indications of success and failure in endeavors

9. ***Mālinī Shāstra*:** Attributed to Sage Rishyashriṅga; a comprehensive treatise dealing with flowers and their arrangements, including making garlands and bouquets, how women can adorn themselves with flowers, conveying messages of love through flowers, etc.

10. ***Malla Shāstra*:** Attributed to Malla Muni; deals with health-preservation and bodybuilding; the science of gymnastics, athletics, wrestling, etc.

11. ***Mahendra Jāla*:** Attributed to Vīrabāhu; deals with the science of magic; describes the art of creating illusions (flying, walking on water, etc.)

12. ***Parakāyā Pravesha*:** Attributed to Valakhilyas; deals with the eight *siddhis*—*aṇimā, mahimā, laghimā, garimā, īshitva, vashitva, prāpti,* and *prakāshya*; the 32 yogas leading to *parakāyā pravesha,* or the transfer of one's *jīva,* at will, to another body (as was done by Ādi Shaṅkara into the body of King Amaruka)

13. ***Ratna Parīkshā and Kanaka Parīkshā*:** Attributed to Sage Vatsyana; deals with the science of testing precious stones and gold for genuineness, including the 24 *lakshaṇā*s (signs) of precious stones and gems, their categorization, and the 32 tests of their quality and genuineness

14. ***Sāmudrika Shāstra*:** Attributed to Samudra Rājā, or Lord Varuṇa; deals with the various body marks that are said to indicate a person's character, life, and experiences; said to have started with Varuṇa's reading of the auspicious marks on Lord Vishṇu's

reclining body; further developed through the later contributions of Nārada, Varāha, Māṇḍavya, etc.; one of its branches is palmistry

15. ***Saudāmini Shāstra*:** Attributed to Sage Mātaṅga of Mount Rishyamukha; deals with *chhāyā-grahaṇa*, or the power and use of shadows; also deals with the science of photography and its derivations

16. ***Shabda Shāstra*:** Attributed to Rishi Kanḍika; deals with sounds and echoes, their categorizations and modifications, and the mechanical reproduction of sounds (pitch, frequency, velocity, etc.)

17. ***Shakti Tantra Shāstra*:** Attributed to Sage Agastya; consists of eight detailed chapters that deal with the various energies and powers in the universe, including the 64 kinds of energy in Nature; the sun, moon, and their *shakti*s; the practical applications to harness such forces; the unlimited energy contained in the atom; an atom's fusion and fission; and nuclear science

18. ***Shilpa Shāstra*:** Attributed to Sage Kashyapa; deals with sculpture, construction of idols, temples, palaces, etc; 22 chapters with 307 categories of sculptures and over 100 types of images and idols, including their dimensions, proportions, and other characteristics; Vishvakarmā is said to have contributed much to the development of this science

19. ***Sūpa Shāstra*:** Attributed to Sukesha; deals with the science of cooking, which Sukesha is said to have perfected to a science; contains various preparations of condiments, pickles, sweets, puddings, cakes; different dishes to suit the tastes of people in different parts of the world; *sūpa* means "broth" (thus the word *soup*)

20. ***Turaṅga Shāstra*:** Comprehensive treatise on horses by Agnivarman; expounds on everything about horses, including breeding, upbringing, pedigree, points for selection, and various

uses, including war; King Nala is also said to have written a treatise called *Ashva Hridaya* on this subject

21. ***Vātāvaraṇa Shāstra*:** Attributed to Sage Atri; deals with clouds, their categorization and characteristics; 12 different kinds of rain; 64 types of lightning; 33 types of thunderbolts, etc.

22. ***Visha Shāstra*:** Attributed to the Ashvini Kumāras; exhaustive treatise on the science of poisons; elaborate discussions about the 32 broad categories of all poisons, including their properties, preparations, applications, and antidotes

23. ***Yantra Shāstra*:** Attributed to Sage Bharadvāja; deals with the types of vehicles for movement on land, water, and air; also deals with the possibility and methodology of movement in space without any vehicle, using only mantras (mystic sound symbols) and *tantra*s (energy forces)

PRAMĀṆAS: MEANS OF KNOWLEDGE

According to Hindu scriptures, the various means or sources of human knowledge are:

- ***Pratyaksha*:** Perception
- ***Anumāna*:** Inference
- ***Āpta Vākya* (*Shabda*):** Testimony (verbal)
- ***Upamāna*:** Comparison
- ***Arthāpatti*:** Postulation
- ***Anupalabdhi*:** Noncognition

Hindu thinkers of different schools of philosophy have varying standpoints on what they accept as valid sources of knowledge.

The *Chārvāka*s admit only one source of valid knowledge: perception.

The *Baudha*s and *Vaisheshika*s admit two sources: perception and inference.

The *Sānkhya*s state three sources: perception, inference, and verbal testimony.

The *Naiyāyika*s also accept a fourth way: comparison.

The *Prabhākara*s add a fifth dimension: postulation or assumption.

The *Bhaṭṭa*s and *Vedāntin*s add a sixth source: noncognition or nonperception. Noncognition is the knowledge of the absence of a thing, such as when we say, "There is no jar in this room." The *Bhaṭṭa*s and *Vedāntin*s thus accept all six sources of knowledge.

108 PRINCIPAL UPANISHADS

From *Rig Veda* (11)

Aitareya

Aksha-mālikā

Ātma-bodha

Bahvricha

Kaushītaki

Mudgala

Nāda-bindu

Nirvāṇa

Sarasvatī-rahasya

Saubhāgya-lakshmī

Tripura

From *Yajur Veda* (*Krishṇa Yajur Veda*) (28)

Akshi

Amrita-bindu (Brahma-bindu)

Amrita-nāda

Avadhūta

Brahma

Brahma-vidyā

Dakshiṇāmūrti

Dhyāna-bindu

Ekākshara

Garbha

Kālāgni-rudra

Kali-santaraṇa

Kaṭha

Kaṭha-rudra

Nārāyaṇa

Pañcha-brahma

Prāṇāgnihotra

Rudra-hridaya

Sarva-sāra

Shārīraka

Shuka-rahasya

Skanda

Taittirīya

Tejobindu

Varāha

Yoga-kuṇḍalinī

Yoga-shikhā

Yoga-tattva

From *Yajur Veda* (*Shukla Yajur Veda*) (21)

Adhyātma

Advaya-tāraka

Bhikshuka

Brihadāraṇyaka

Haṁsa

Īshāvāsya

Jābāla

Kshurikā

Maṇḍala-brāhmaṇa

Māntrika

Muktika

Nirālamba

Paiṅgala

Paramahaṁsa

Shātyāyana

Subālā

Svetāshvatara

Tārasāra

Trisikha

Turīyātīta

Yājñavalkya

From *Sāma Veda* (16)

Āruṇeya

Avyakta

Chhāndogya

Darshana

Jābāla

Kena

Kuṇḍika

Mahā

Maitrāyaṇī

Maitreya

Rudrāksha

Sannyāsa

Sāvitrī

Vajrasūchī

Vāsudeva

Yoga-chūḍāmaṇi

From *Atharva Veda* (32)

Annapūrṇa

Atharva-shikhā

Atharva-shira

Ātma

Bhasma-jābāla

Bhāvanā

Brihajjābāla

Dattātreya

Devī

Gaṇapati

Gāruḍa

Gopāla-tāpanī

Hayagrīva

*Kaivalya**

Krishṇa

Mahānārāyaṇa

Mahāvākya

Māṇḍūkya

Muṇḍaka

Nārada-parivrājaka

Nrisiṁha-tāpanī

Parabrahma

Paramahaṁsa-parivrājaka

Pāshupata

Prashna

Rāma-rahasya

Rāma-tāpanī

Shāṇḍilya

Sharabha

Sītā

Sūrya

Tripura-tāpanī

* Some sources list *Kaivalya Upanishad* under *Krishṇa Yajur Veda.*

NOTE: The information given in the Appendix has been compiled from various sources and has not been verified. Please refer to direct sources for further study.

SANSKRIT PRONUNCIATION GUIDE

a	fun	**i**	pin	**om**	**foam**
ā	car	**ī**	feet	**p**	**p**urse
ai	high	**j**	**j**ug	**ph**	sap**ph**ire
au	cow	**jh**	he**dgeh**og	**r**	**r**un
b	**but**	**jñ**	*no equivalent*	**ṛ**	rig
bh	a**bh**or	**k**	**k**ind	**ṝ**	*long* **ṛ**
c	**ch**unk	**kh**	bloc**kh**ead	**s**	**s**ir
ch	mat**ch**	**kṣ**	wor**ksh**eet	**ś**	**sh**ovel
d	fea**th**er	**l**	**l**uck	**ṣ**	bu**sh**el
dh	wi**th**er	**ḷ**	world	**t**	**th**ink
ḍ	**d**uck	**m**	mother	**th**	pa**th**etic
ḍh	go**d-h**ood	**ṃ**	*see below*	**ṭ**	touch
e	play	**n**	**n**umber	**ṭh**	an**th**ill
g	**g**ate	**ṇ**	thunder	**tr**	**thr**ee
gh	lo**g-h**ut	**ṅ**	si**ng**	**u**	put
h	**h**ouse	**ñ**	bunch	**ū**	pool
ḥ	*see below*	**o**	over	**v**	**v**irtue
				y	**y**oung

ḥ	aspiration of preceding vowel
ṃ	nasalization of preceding vowel
’	unprounounced **a**
”	unprounounced **ā**